It's another Quality Book from CGP

Grammar, Punctuation and Spelling are really important in
Key Stage 2 English (ages 7-11)... and there's plenty to learn.

Happily, this CGP book explains everything as clearly and simply
as possible, with plenty of helpful examples along the way.

It's also fully up-to-date for the latest curriculum changes,
making it ideal for the SATS.

What CGP is all about

Our sole aim here at CGP is to produce the highest quality
books — carefully written, immaculately presented and
dangerously close to being funny.

Then we work our socks off to get them out to you
— at the cheapest possible prices.

Contents

SECTION THREE — PUNCTUATION

SECTION FOUR — SPELLING

Published by CGP

From original material by Richard Parsons

Editors:
Heather Gregson
Rachel Grocott
Sabrina Robinson
Rebecca Tate

With thanks to Anthony Muller for the proofreading.

ISBN: 978 1 84762 165 8

Clipart from Corel®
Printed by Elanders Ltd, Newcastle upon Tyne.

Nouns

Nouns are <u>naming words</u>. You need to know <u>what they are</u>, and be able to <u>spot them</u> in a sentence.

Common nouns **are** things

Common nouns are <u>straight-forward</u>, <u>everyday</u> words for <u>things</u>. They can be <u>singular</u> or <u>plural</u>.

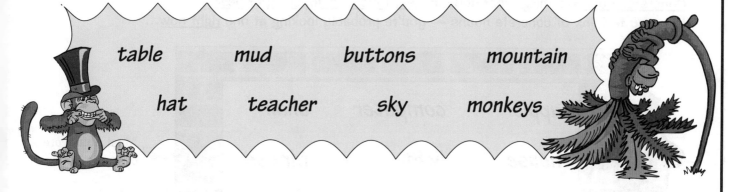

table   mud   buttons   mountain

hat   teacher   sky   monkeys

Proper nouns **are** names

Proper nouns are names for <u>particular people</u>, <u>places</u> or <u>things</u>, like <u>days</u> or <u>months</u>.
Proper nouns <u>always</u> need a <u>capital letter</u>. Don't you forget it...

February   *Brazil*   *Penny Lane*

Wednesday   *River Thames*

Bristol   *Robert*   *Queen Victoria*

Collective nouns **are for** groups

Collective nouns are special names for <u>groups</u> of things.

flock   herd   pack

team   swarm   crowd

There are loads of collective nouns for groups of animals. E.g. a <u>pride</u> of lions, a <u>gaggle</u> of geese...

Nouns

Nouns can be <u>concrete</u> or <u>abstract</u>. Abstract nouns are slightly <u>trickier</u> to remember, so <u>learn the examples</u> on this page and try to think of some more of your own.

Concrete nouns _are things you_ can touch

<u>Concrete nouns</u> are things that you can <u>see</u>, <u>touch</u>, <u>taste</u>, <u>smell</u> or <u>hear</u>.
It's easy to think of concrete nouns — you're probably looking at one <u>right now</u>...

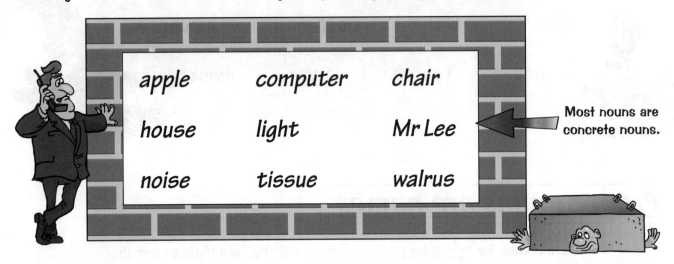

apple	computer	chair
house	light	Mr Lee
noise	tissue	walrus

Most nouns are concrete nouns.

Abstract nouns _are for_ ideas _and_ concepts

<u>Abstract nouns</u> are things you can't <u>see</u>, <u>touch</u>, <u>taste</u>, <u>smell</u> or <u>hear</u>.
<u>Ideas</u> and <u>emotions</u> are abstract nouns.

education   friendship   childhood

courage   fear   excellence   beauty

happiness   politeness   curiosity

Quick Questions...

Write out the nouns below then say whether each one is common, proper, collective or abstract.
1) As Kai stood on Brighton Pier, a flock of seagulls swooped down and stole his doughnuts.
2) The superstar needed inspiration, so she jumped on a plane and went to Barbados.

Pronouns

Once <u>you</u> start looking for <u>them</u>, <u>you'll</u> realise that <u>you</u> use pronouns <u>all</u> the time.

Pronouns <u>replace a noun</u>

1) <u>Pronouns</u> save you from <u>repeating a noun</u> over and over again. They're really pretty <u>nifty</u>.

> Marc said <u>he</u> would bring the doughnuts, but <u>he</u> forgot <u>them</u>.

'<u>He</u>' is a pronoun which replaces the name '<u>Marc</u>'.

'<u>Them</u>' is a pronoun which replaces '<u>the doughnuts</u>'.

2) Take <u>care</u> with pronouns — sometimes it's not <u>clear</u> who you're talking about:

> April cooked her mum a meal and <u>she</u> thought it was fantastic.

It's not clear <u>who</u> thought the meal was fantastic.

These are the <u>main pronouns</u>

There are <u>two</u> groups of pronouns, and you need to learn both really well.
If you don't use the <u>right one</u> your sentences won't make <u>sense</u>. See p.26 for more.

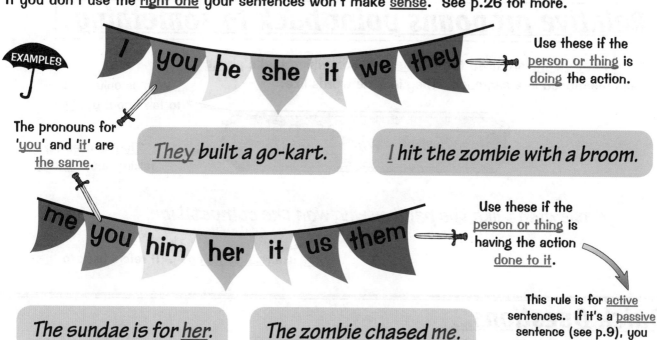

EXAMPLES

I you he she it we they

Use these if the <u>person or thing</u> is <u>doing</u> the action.

The pronouns for '<u>you</u>' and '<u>it</u>' are <u>the same</u>.

<u>They</u> built a go-kart.

<u>I</u> hit the zombie with a broom.

me you him her it us them

Use these if the <u>person or thing</u> is having the action <u>done to it</u>.

The sundae is for <u>her</u>.

The zombie chased <u>me</u>.

This rule is for <u>active</u> sentences. If it's a <u>passive</u> sentence (see p.9), you need to <u>swap</u> the <u>pronoun types</u> round, e.g. 'I was chased by the zombie.'

Pronouns

Oh yes, there are <u>more pronouns</u> to be learnt. They're <u>useful little things</u> though, I promise.

Some pronouns show belonging

Some pronouns show <u>who</u> owns something. These are called '<u>possessive pronouns</u>'. Here they are:

mine	*yours*	*his*	*hers*	*ours*	*theirs*

"Whose skis are these?" I asked.
"They're <u>mine</u>," said Peter.

'<u>Mine</u>' is a <u>possessive pronoun</u> which saves you from saying '<u>my skis</u>'.

'<u>Hers</u>' is a <u>possessive pronoun</u> which saves you from saying '<u>her scooter</u>'.

Omar didn't have a scooter, so <u>he</u> borrowed <u>hers</u>.

Sentences often have <u>more than one</u> pronoun.

Relative pronouns point back to something

<u>Relative pronouns</u> are used to <u>refer back</u> to something that's <u>already</u> been mentioned in a sentence. They include words like:

which	who	that

'<u>Who</u>' is only used to talk about <u>people</u>.

'<u>That</u>' is used for talking about <u>things</u>.

Katie didn't like the painter <u>who</u> won the competition.

'<u>Who</u>' is a <u>relative pronoun</u>. It refers back to <u>the painter</u>.

Quick Questions...

Copy each sentence and underline all the pronouns.
1) "Dad," I said, "the slippers are yours."
2) Ganika said she would be late for school.
3) We took the parcel and hid it under the bed.
4) Hal has sweets that he won't share.

Determiners

Determiners are <u>small words</u> that go before <u>nouns</u>. Tricky blighters, these ones...

Articles are 'a', 'an' or 'the'

An <u>article</u> is one <u>type</u> of determiner. The words '<u>a</u>', '<u>an</u>' and '<u>the</u>' are all <u>articles</u>.
Use '<u>a</u>' and '<u>an</u>' for <u>general</u> things and '<u>the</u>' for <u>specific</u> things.

Leonora spoke to <u>a</u> ghost.

This could be <u>any ghost</u>.

Leonora spoke to <u>the</u> ghost.

This means a <u>specific ghost</u>.

Use '<u>a</u>' when the next word starts with a <u>consonant</u> sound, and
'<u>an</u>' when the next word starts with a <u>vowel</u> sound.

Vowel sounds are usually
made by the letters
'a', 'e', 'i', 'o' and 'u'.

<u>a</u> garage

<u>an</u> alligator

These ones are easy-peasy:
'g' is a <u>consonant sound</u> and
'<u>a</u>' is a <u>vowel sound</u>.

<u>a</u> university

This one's trickier — 'university' starts with a <u>vowel</u> ('<u>u</u>') but it <u>sounds like</u>
it could start with a '<u>y</u>'. This is a <u>consonant sound</u>, so it goes with '<u>a</u>'.

Here are some other types of determiner

There are <u>lots</u> more types of determiner, which all have different <u>jobs</u> to do in a sentence.

1) They can show whether a noun is <u>specific</u> or <u>general</u>:

I bought <u>some</u> cheese.

This could be <u>any cheese</u>.

The hen laid <u>this</u> egg.

This means a <u>specific egg</u>.

2) They can show <u>how many</u> things there are:

He had <u>three</u> mice.

3) They can show who <u>owns</u> something:

Sam had found <u>her</u> books.

Quick Questions...

Copy each sentence and circle all the determiners.
1) Could you please pass me some sprouts?
2) I have an aunt called Lou from Timbuktu.
3) The police officer was my hero.
4) For the pie I need fourteen onions.

<u>Verbs</u>

Verbs are <u>important</u> because they tell you <u>what's happening</u> in a sentence. In fact, if it <u>doesn't</u> have a verb, it's <u>not a sentence</u> at all. All the more reason to learn these pages...

<u>Verbs are doing or being words</u>

Verbs are <u>action</u> words — they show what a person or thing is <u>doing</u> or <u>being</u>.

I <u>am</u> an artist.

The girl <u>talks</u> loudly.

> Sentences can have <u>more than one</u> verb. See p.8 for more.

They <u>wear</u> funny clothes.

Arun <u>is building</u> a rocket.

Whoever's <u>doing the verb</u> in a sentence is <u>the subject</u>.

> It's different for <u>passive</u> sentences though. See p.9.

<u>The girl</u> talks loudly.

<u>Arun</u> is building a rocket.

'The girl' is the <u>subject</u>.

'Arun' is the <u>subject</u>.

<u>The subject</u> and the <u>verb</u> have to <u>agree</u>

<u>Verbs change</u> depending on <u>who's</u> doing the action.

<u>I look</u> confused.

<u>It looks</u> confused.

> Most verbs stay the same if 'I', 'you', 'we' or 'they' are doing the action, but they change for 'he', 'she' and 'it'.

<u>She sells</u> seashells.

<u>They sell</u> seashells.

<u>He tries</u> the strange sandwiches.

<u>We try</u> the strange sandwiches.

Verbs

Verb tenses tell you if an action takes place in the <u>past</u>, the <u>present</u> or the <u>future</u>.

Verb tenses tell you when

1) The tense of a verb tells you <u>when</u> something happens. The verb <u>changes</u> in the different tenses.

I <u>talked</u>.

You can often add <u>-ed</u> to the verb to make it <u>past tense</u>. (See p.53).

I <u>talk</u>.

This is the <u>present tense</u>.

I <u>will talk</u>.

You can put '<u>will</u>' in front of the verb to make the <u>future tense</u>.

2) The <u>past tense</u> can be <u>tricky</u> to form.
<u>Not all</u> verbs follow the '<u>add -ed</u>' rule. Take these, for example:

Present	go	eat	take	do	have	see	think	speak	come
Past	went	ate	took	did	had	saw	thought	spoke	came

3) It's really <u>important</u> that you use the <u>right tense</u> in your writing. If you start writing about something in the <u>past tense</u>, then make sure you <u>carry on</u> writing in the <u>past tense</u>.

Use 'to be' with -ing verbs

1) To show an action is <u>currently happening</u>, you use the <u>present progressive</u> form. This is made using part of the verb '<u>to be</u>' (see p.24) and an <u>-ing</u> verb. The verb 'to be' is a <u>helping verb</u>. It tells you <u>more</u> about the -ing verb.

We <u>are flying</u> to Mars.

The part of '<u>to be</u>' ('<u>are</u>') is in the <u>present tense</u>. This means that the -ing verb is <u>happening right now</u>.

The -ing part tells you <u>what</u> the action is.

2) You can also use '<u>to be</u>' in the <u>past</u> tense to make the <u>past progressive</u> form.

We <u>were flying</u> to Mars.

'<u>Were</u>' is the helping verb. It's in the <u>past tense</u>. This means the action was happening <u>in the past</u>.

Quick Questions...

Copy out these sentences and correct the verbs so that they agree with the subject.
1) The dog eat my homework.
2) They wants ice cream for pudding.
3) You is doing the washing up tonight.
4) I often thinks before I speaks.

Verbs

You know those 'helping' verbs you read about on p.7? Here are some more of them. They're really important. Some sentences won't even make sense if you don't use them.

You can use 'have' to make the perfect form

1) To talk about things that have already happened, you can use the present tense of 'have'.

> This is the present perfect form.

> *I have finished the book.*

> For more about 'been' and 'done' with 'have', see p.25.

In this sentence, 'have' is the helping verb.

The writer has already read the book. This verb is in the past tense.

2) To talk about something that happened before something else, you can use the past tense of 'have'.

> *We had done our homework, so the lesson was easy.*

> This is the past perfect form.

This helping verb is different — it's in the past tense.

By the time of the lesson, the children had already done their homework.

3) The part after 'had' or 'have' is often the same as the normal past tense, but not always. You just need to learn the ones that are different.

> *He has spoke to the class.* ✗

> *You have ate the apple.* ✗

This should be 'spoken'.

This should be 'eaten'.

Some helping verbs show possibility

Words like 'should' and 'would' are called modal verbs. They can show how likely an action is.

> *We could sing at your party.*

'Could' is the modal verb.

'Sing' is the main verb. This is the bit of the verb you'd find in the dictionary.

> *I might borrow her stilts.*

'Might' is the modal verb.

'Should' is the modal verb.

> *You should bring your bug collection.*

Verbs

Active and passive verbs are two ways of giving the same information. Study this page until you can tell one from the other — like a grammatical 'spot the difference'.

Active sentences focus on who

Most sentences are in the active voice — it's clear who is doing the action (the subject). The verb agrees with the person doing the action (see p.6).

Prajesh flipped the pancake.

Prajesh is doing
the action.
He's the subject.

The pancake is having
the action done to it.
It's the object.

Kev and Don built the house five years ago.

Kev and Don are
the subjects.

The house (the object) is
having the action done to it.

Passive sentences focus on what

When a sentence is in the passive voice, something is done to the subject.

 EXAMPLES

The pancake was flipped by Prajesh.

the subject

The word 'by' can introduce
who does the action.

The house was built by Kev and Don five years ago.

the subject

You don't always need to say who does the
action in passive sentences. 'The house was
built five years ago' makes sense too.

Quick Questions...

Decide whether each sentence below is active or passive.
1) My neighbours threw a massive party.
2) The soup was served in teapots.
3) The puppy was left by the side of the road.
4) The painting was done by her sister.

Adjectives

Adjectives are <u>describing</u> words. Without them, everything would sound <u>really boring</u>.

Adjectives describe a noun

You need to be able to spot an <u>adjective</u> in a sentence.
Just remember, it's always the word that is <u>describing</u> the <u>noun</u>.

Colin's head is <u>massive</u>.

Granny's T.V. is <u>ancient</u>.

These words are all <u>adjectives</u>.

I love <u>greasy</u> burgers.

The <u>icy</u> rain soaked us.

Remember that <u>more than one</u> adjective can <u>describe</u> a noun.

The creature was <u>ugly</u> and <u>strange</u>.

You can use '<u>and</u>' to
separate adjectives...

...or you can use <u>commas</u>.
See p.38.

Jabari hid from the <u>ugly</u>, <u>strange</u> creature.

I didn't see <u>the ugly, strange</u>
<u>creature with red eyes</u>.

'<u>The ugly, strange creature</u>' is a <u>noun phrase</u>.
A noun phrase is a group of words which includes
a <u>noun</u> and any words that <u>describe</u> it.

You can add <u>adjectives</u>, <u>prepositions</u> or
other nouns to <u>expand</u> a noun phrase.

Learn where adjectives go in a sentence

Adjectives can come right <u>before</u> the noun, like this:

The <u>sleepy</u> dragon guarded her <u>valuable</u> treasure.

Here, both adjectives come
<u>before</u> the nouns they describe.

They <u>don't always</u> go <u>next to</u> the word <u>they're describing</u>:

The dragon's treasure was <u>gold</u> and <u>shiny</u>.

Here, the adjectives
come <u>after</u> the noun.

Adjectives

Adjectives can also be used to compare things. Useful, right?

Say that something is more or less

Adjectives can tell you if something is bigger, better, smaller and so on. These adjectives are called 'comparatives'.

Kwesi's bike is newer.

With short adjectives, you can often add -er on the end to make them comparatives. For spelling changes with 'er' see p.52.

My trousers are brighter than yours.

These common comparatives are irregular:
good → better → the best
bad → worse → the worst

Magda is less generous than Sian.

With longer adjectives you need to use the words 'more' or 'less'.

My poodle is more elegant than your bulldog.

Say that something is the best or the worst

Adjectives can show you that something is the most, least, best or worst out of a group. These types of adjectives are called 'superlatives'.

His backpack is the lightest.

You can add -est to short adjectives to make them mean 'the most' or 'the least'.

1324 x 6 =

Cosmo is the most popular kid at school.

For longer adjectives you need to write 'the most / the least' + adjective.

Quick Questions...

Write out all the adjectives in these sentences. Underline any that are superlatives.
1) I love cold ice-cream on a hot day.   3) Of all the stinky shoes, yours are the stinkiest.
2) This is the funniest film I've ever seen.   4) Brian's unusual hat was green and orange.

Adverbs

Adverbs <u>describe</u> verbs. They <u>add</u> to the <u>verb</u> — <u>adverb</u>. Bet you didn't see that one coming.

Adverbs *describe verbs*

<u>Adverbs</u> tell you <u>how</u> or <u>when</u> an action was done. Often, adverbs end in '<u>-ly</u>'.

The stars shone <u>brightly</u>. '<u>Brightly</u>' is the adverb. It tells you <u>how</u> the stars shone.

Dad was sleeping <u>peacefully</u>. '<u>Peacefully</u>' is the adverb.

Irfan arrived <u>late</u>. '<u>Late</u>' is the adverb. Not all adverbs end in '<u>-ly</u>'.

Sometimes, <u>a group of words</u> tells you how the action was done. This is called an '<u>adverbial phrase</u>'.

Mario ate his pasta <u>as quickly as he could</u>.

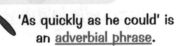

'As quickly as he could' is an <u>adverbial phrase</u>.

Adverbs also *describe adjectives*

Words like '<u>very</u>', '<u>quite</u>' and '<u>extremely</u>' and '<u>nearly</u>' are also <u>adverbs</u>. They can be used with <u>adjectives</u> to show <u>how much</u> the adjective is working on the noun.

Fido's hat is <u>quite</u> big.   *Fido's hat is <u>extremely</u> big.*

Adverbs <u>always</u> come before the adjective they're describing.

This kind of adverb can also describe <u>other adverbs</u>:

She plays <u>really confidently</u>. '<u>Really</u>' is an adverb working on the adverb '<u>confidently</u>'.

Matt waited <u>very patiently</u>. '<u>Very</u>' is an adverb working on the adverb '<u>patiently</u>'.

Adverbs

Oh yeah, <u>more</u> stuff on adverbs. Learn it all <u>carefully</u> (there's another adverb for you).

Adverbs can go before or after a verb

Look at these <u>examples</u> to see how adverbs can go <u>before</u> or <u>after</u> the verb in your sentence.

The fish swam along <u>happily</u>.

The shark <u>secretly</u> followed.

<u>Adverbs</u> can also go at the <u>start</u> of a sentence. See p.23.

<u>Perhaps</u> he was waiting for his dinner.

Adverbs like '<u>perhaps</u>' and '<u>probably</u>' show how <u>likely</u> something is.

Don't get adverbs and adjectives confused

1) <u>Not all</u> words that <u>end</u> in <u>-ly</u> are adverbs. Sometimes this can be a bit <u>tricky</u>...

'Friendly' and 'lovely' are words that end in -ly but they are <u>adjectives</u>, <u>not adverbs</u>.

2) Some words can be an <u>adverb</u> or an <u>adjective</u>, depending on the sentence. For example, words like '<u>late</u>', '<u>hard</u>', '<u>low</u>', and '<u>most</u>'.

Gerald loves <u>fast</u> cars.

In this sentence, '<u>fast</u>' is an <u>adjective</u> because it is describing the noun '<u>cars</u>'.

That chicken can run <u>fast</u>!

In this sentence, '<u>fast</u>' is an <u>adverb</u> because it is describing the verb '<u>run</u>'.

Quick Questions...

Write out these sentences and underline all of the adverbs.

1) The friendly aliens visit Earth frequently.
2) The fireworks exploded extremely brightly.
3) The giraffe was snoring incredibly loudly.
4) She worked hard to finish the hard sums.

Prepositions

Prepositions tell you how things are related to one another.
They tell you where things are or when things happen, in relation to one another.

Prepositions can tell you where

Some prepositions tell you where things are in relation to other things in the sentence.

> under   over   at   on   in   through   into

EXAMPLES

I stuffed the sweets <u>into</u> my pocket.

'Into' shows where the sweets are in relation to the pocket.

He hid the money <u>under</u> the bed.

There was a vampire <u>at</u> the party.

Prepositions can tell you when

Other prepositions tell you when things happen in relation to each other.

> while   during   until   since   in   before   after

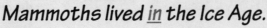

I fell asleep <u>during</u> the cricket.

Mammoths lived <u>in</u> the Ice Age.

The soldiers marched <u>until</u> 10 o'clock.

Prepositions

This page has some fiddly stuff on it, but it's nothing you can't handle.
Learn the rule and go over the examples until you're sure you've got it nailed.

Prepositions are often followed by a noun

Prepositions show how words are related, e.g. how one noun is related to another noun.
In this case, one of the nouns comes after the preposition.

The preposition 'under'
shows where the cat hid
in relation to the table.

The cat hid under the table.

preposition   noun

Sometimes, a noun phrase follows a preposition. A noun phrase is a noun
plus any other words that give more information about the noun.

The knight rode on the brown cow.

preposition   noun phrase

The preposition 'on' shows
where the knight rode in
relation to the brown cow.

Pronouns can follow prepositions

Prepositions can also show how a pronoun is related to something else.

The house is behind you.

preposition   pronoun

The preposition 'behind' shows where
the house is in relation to you.

Nikki left after them.

preposition   pronoun

The preposition 'after' shows when
Nikki left in relation to them.

Quick Questions...

Choose a suitable preposition to complete each sentence.
1) I carry my books ___ my school bag.
2) Matt eats breakfast ___ he gets dressed.
3) I have not seen him ___ last week.
4) The car drove ___ the bridge.

Test-Style Questions

You can <u>bet your boots</u> that there will be a question about <u>word types</u> in your <u>SATs</u>. Have a go at these <u>practice questions</u> to make sure you're <u>prepared</u>.

Here's a Practice Question

Follow these <u>simple steps</u> for working out <u>the answer</u> to a question about <u>word types</u>:

1. Look at the table below. <u>Put a tick in each row</u> to show whether the word is an **adverb** or an **adjective**.

This tells you what you need to do.

'Gently' is an adverb. It describes verbs, e.g. 'stroke gently'.

'Lovely' ends in '-ly' but it's an adjective, e.g. 'a lovely day' (see p.13).

Word	Adverb	Adjective
gently	✓	
lovely		✓
funny		✓

'Funny' is an adjective. It describes nouns, e.g. 'the funny actor'.

Test-Style Questions

The answers are on p.66, but don't be a cheetah!

Now have a go at some <u>questions</u> by <u>yourself</u>.

1. Read the sentence below and circle all the **determiners**.

   At the circus I saw a tightrope walker and two escape artists.

2. Read the sentence below.
   Circle the most suitable **pronoun** to complete the sentence.

   When my sister and I finish school, _____ go

   straight to grandma's house.

   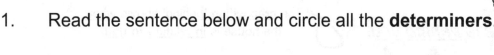

   she   we   they   us

Test-Style Questions

3. Put a letter in each box to show which **word class** the words belong to.

noun A	verb B	adjective C	adverb D

Of all my shoes, my oldest ones fit me most comfortably.

↑ ☐ ↑ ☐ ↑ ☐ ↑ ☐

4. Read the passage below. Change all the underlined verbs from the **present** tense to the **past** tense.

One has already been done for you.

gave
↑

In class today I <u>give</u> a talk about my school project.

☐   ☐
↑   ↑

I <u>speak</u> to the class about the Tudors and I <u>tell</u> them about

☐
↑

Henry VIII's six wives. The talk <u>is</u> a great success.

5. Read the sentences below.
Write a different **adverb** in each space.

The ballerina danced _____ across the stage and

the audience clapped _____ .

Sentences

Now you've looked at types of <u>words</u>, it's time to look at types of <u>sentences</u>. These neat little collections of words come in lots of <u>shapes</u> and <u>sizes</u>, so you need to get your head round them.

Statements *usually give* information

1) <u>Statements</u> are sentences which <u>tell</u> you something.

2) The <u>word types</u> in a statement are usually in the <u>same order</u>:

The <u>subject</u> usually comes <u>first</u> (the person or thing doing the verb).

Statements <u>end</u> with a <u>full stop</u>.

For more on active and passive verbs, see p.9.

> The alien   eats   the cheese.

The <u>verb</u> comes next.

The <u>object</u> usually comes <u>after</u> the verb. It's the person or thing that the verb is being <u>done to</u>.

3) You can make statements <u>more complicated</u> by adding other <u>types</u> of words.

> The <u>huge</u> alien eats the cheese <u>hungrily</u>.

adjective   adverb

For other <u>word types</u>, see Section One.

Questions *always ask about something*

Questions often start with a <u>question word</u>.

> who   what   when   where   why   how   which

Most <u>question words</u> start with a '<u>w</u>'.

> <u>Who</u> is taking the rabbit for a walk<u>?</u>

Questions are <u>easy</u> to spot — they <u>always</u> end in a <u>question mark</u> (see p.32).

Sometimes statements can be <u>rearranged</u> to make questions:

> <u>They are</u> hungry.   <u>Are they</u> hungry<u>?</u>

pronoun   verb   verb   pronoun

Questions like this <u>don't</u> need a question word, but they do need a <u>question mark</u>.

In <u>informal writing</u> (e.g. if you were writing to a friend), <u>question tags</u> are sometimes used:

> It's a nice day outside, <u>isn't it</u>?

The question tag '<u>isn't it</u>' turns this sentence into a <u>question</u>.

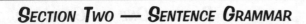

Sentences

Ok, so that's the easy ones out of the way — <u>statements</u> and <u>questions</u> should have been on your radar for years. <u>Commands</u> and <u>exclamations</u> are a little trickier, so hold onto your hats.

Commands *give* instructions *or* orders

1) Commands tell people <u>what to do</u>.

> <u>Don't</u> run!   Please <u>go</u> away.   <u>Stop</u> it!

Commands can end in an <u>exclamation mark</u> or a <u>full stop</u>. Use an <u>exclamation mark</u> for <u>strong</u> or <u>urgent</u> commands.

2) <u>Commands</u> always have a <u>verb</u> that gives an <u>order</u>:

These are the <u>verbs</u> that give the <u>order</u>.

> <u>Look</u> behind you!
> <u>Turn</u> around!
> <u>Put</u> the cake in the oven.

3) Sometimes you can <u>turn a question</u> into a <u>command</u>:

> Can you make the dinner? ⟶ Make the dinner!

Exclamations **show** strong feelings

1) Exclamations show <u>strong feelings</u> like surprise, pain, anger or excitement.
2) They <u>always</u> start with either '<u>what</u>' or '<u>how</u>'.
3) They are always proper <u>sentences</u> — they have to have a <u>verb</u>.

EXAMPLES

> What a great idea that was!   How strangely he sings!

> Exclamations <u>always</u> have an <u>exclamation mark</u>.

Quick Questions...

Write down whether each sentence is a statement, question, command or exclamation.
1) What bad luck that was!   3) Put it down!   5) Please don't talk.   7) Is he ill?
2) Where are the ants?   4) I don't like it.   6) How quickly he runs!   8) You're asleep.

Phrases and Clauses

I'll be honest — these two pages aren't the <u>easiest</u> ones in this book. But there's a fish on a bicycle to help you understand the difference between <u>phrases</u> and <u>clauses</u>. What more could you want?

Sentences <u>are</u> made of <u>phrases</u> <u>and</u> <u>clauses</u>

A <u>clause</u> is part of a sentence which has <u>a subject</u> and <u>a verb</u>.

Jonas rides his bike at the circus.

This is a <u>clause</u> because it has a <u>verb</u> ('<u>rides</u>') and a <u>subject</u> ('<u>Jonas</u>').

A <u>phrase</u> is part of a sentence, usually <u>without a verb</u>.

Jonas rides his bike <u>at the circus</u>.

This is a <u>phrase</u>. It doesn't have a verb.

Sometimes phrases <u>can</u> have a <u>verb</u>, but there <u>won't</u> be <u>anyone</u> doing the verb (<u>a subject</u>). E.g. '<u>riding a bike</u>' is a phrase.

<u>Two</u> main clauses <u>make a</u> compound sentence

1) A <u>main clause</u> is a clause that would <u>make sense</u> as a <u>separate sentence</u>.

2) A <u>compound sentence</u> is made of <u>two main clauses</u> which are <u>equally important</u>.

3) Main clauses are joined by a <u>word</u> like '<u>and</u>', '<u>or</u>' or '<u>but</u>'. These are <u>conjunctions</u> (see p.22-23).

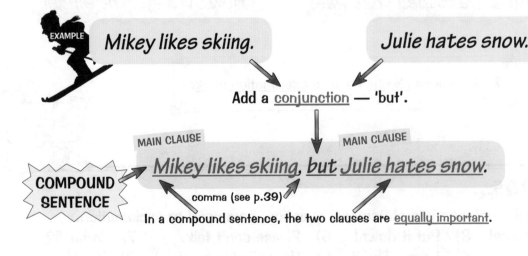

EXAMPLE

Mikey likes skiing.   **Julie hates snow.**

Add a <u>conjunction</u> — 'but'.

MAIN CLAUSE   MAIN CLAUSE

<u>Mikey likes skiing</u>, <u>but</u> <u>Julie hates snow</u>.

COMPOUND SENTENCE

comma (see p.39)

In a compound sentence, the two clauses are <u>equally important</u>.

Phrases and Clauses

You should know the difference between a <u>clause</u> and a <u>phrase</u> by now. If you've forgotten, take a look back at the last page pronto, because now it's time to cover <u>different types of clause</u>.

Complex sentences <u>have</u> subordinate clauses

1) A <u>complex sentence</u> has a <u>main clause</u> and a <u>less important</u> clause.
2) The less important clause is called a <u>subordinate clause</u>.
3) <u>Subordinate clauses</u> start with <u>conjunctions</u> like '<u>while</u>', '<u>until</u>' or '<u>because</u>'.
4) Subordinate clauses <u>don't make sense</u> on their <u>own</u>.

> A subordinate clause can also be called a <u>dependent clause</u>.

<u>The old computer attacked</u> <u>while Bob was sleeping</u>.

main clause   subordinate clause

COMPLEX SENTENCE

5) Sometimes the subordinate clause comes <u>before</u> the main clause:

<u>While Bob was sleeping</u>, <u>the old computer attacked</u>.

subordinate clause   You need a comma here (see p.39).   main clause

For more <u>conjunctions</u>, see p.22-23.

Relative clauses <u>give</u> extra information

1) A <u>relative clause</u> is a type of subordinate clause that gives <u>extra information</u> about a <u>noun</u>.
2) <u>Relative pronouns</u> (see p.4) can introduce relative clauses. They include:

> who   which   whose   that

There's the bear <u>that</u> <u>doesn't like bees</u>.

relative pronoun

This is the <u>relative clause</u>. It gives you some <u>extra information</u> about the <u>noun</u> — the bear.

Pablo is a beekeeper <u>who</u> <u>lives next door to the bear</u>.

relative pronoun   relative clause

Quick Questions...

For each sentence, write down whether the underlined part is a main or a subordinate clause.
1) <u>I play chess</u>, and Will plays squash.
2) <u>While Mark was snoring</u>, Millie took a photo of him.
3) He didn't stop <u>until he'd finished</u>.
4) I was scared, but <u>I carried on</u>.

Conjunctions

Conjunctions are the cool little words or phrases which connect words together to make sentences. They can also link sentences to each other to make text flow better. Pretty snazzy, eh?

Conjunctions *join bits of text together*

1) Conjunctions join clauses together to make a sentence.
2) They can also link sentences to each other in a piece of writing.

one bit of text — conjunction — another bit of text

Conjunctions *can join clauses in a sentence*

1) Conjunctions join two main clauses in a compound sentence (see p.20).

COMPOUND SENTENCE

Blue frogs like snow, <u>but</u> they hate mud.

This conjunction joins the two clauses together into one sentence.

It looked slimy, <u>so</u> I didn't touch it.

They can jump really high, <u>yet</u> they only have tiny legs.

Some co-ordinating conjunctions
so   or   yet
and   but

2) Some conjunctions can join a main clause and a subordinate clause in a complex sentence (see p.21).

subordinate clause

I stared silently (because) it was singing.

This conjunction shows that a subordinate clause is about to begin.

COMPLEX SENTENCE

I watched it <u>until</u> it hopped away.

It hid in the bushes <u>while</u> my brother looked for it.

Some subordinating conjunctions
although
until   if
while   because

Conjunctions

Oh, so you thought that last page was <u>all</u> you needed to know about <u>conjunctions</u>, did you?
Well, I've got news for you, buster — there's <u>more</u> where that came from. In fact, it's right here...

Conjunctions can link sentences in a text

Conjunctions like '<u>however</u>', '<u>furthermore</u>', '<u>therefore</u>', '<u>nevertheless</u>'
and '<u>meanwhile</u>' can <u>link sentences</u> together in a text.

> *Sebastien's family thought he was a blackbird.*
> <u>*However*</u>*, he was green, not black.* <u>*Furthermore*</u>*,*
> *he had a large pink feather on his head.*

Sometimes <u>adverbs</u> can be used to <u>link sentences</u> together:

'<u>Suddenly</u>' is an <u>adverb</u>
(see p.12-13).

> *Marcus sniffed.* <u>*Suddenly*</u>*, he was feeling*
> *very hungry. He went through to the kitchen.*
> <u>*Perhaps*</u> *the soup would be ready to eat.*

<u>Adverbs</u> like '<u>perhaps</u>'
show how <u>possible</u>
or <u>likely</u> something
is to happen.

Phrases can also connect sentences

Some types of <u>phrases</u> can <u>act</u> like conjunctions:

<u>Adverbial phrases</u> describe the verb.

> every day, more importantly,
> as soon as possible

<u>Preposition phrases</u> contain prepositions.

> <u>in</u> other words,
> <u>on</u> the other hand

<u>In spite of</u> my
hunger, I'm
quite friendly.

> *The giraffe waited.* <u>*Every day*</u>*, she got hungrier and hungrier.*

adverbial phrase

> *She loved carrots.* <u>*On the other hand*</u>*, she hated sprouts.*

preposition phrase

Quick Questions...

Rewrite each sentence and underline the conjunction:
1) I ate all the pizza, yet I don't like cheese.
2) She went to the cinema because she likes films.
3) He was ill. Nevertheless, he went out.
4) Suddenly, the door creaked open.

Standard and Non-Standard English

Standard English is formal English. It's the type of writing you should use in your written work. And — you guessed it — non-Standard English is a more informal type of English.

The subject and the verb have to agree

In Standard English, the verb in a sentence has to agree with whoever's doing the action. See p.6 for more on verbs and subjects.

She <u>swim</u> every day. ✗
non-Standard English

She <u>swims</u> every day. ✓
Standard English

I <u>has</u> a cowardly cat. ✗

I <u>have</u> a cowardly cat. ✓

It <u>go</u> very fast. ✗

It <u>goes</u> very fast. ✓

They <u>does</u> lots of cleaning. ✗

They <u>do</u> lots of cleaning. ✓

'To be' has to agree with the subject

1) Some verbs don't follow the normal pattern. They're called irregular verbs.
2) The verb '<u>to be</u>' is one of the most common ones, so it's worth learning how it goes.

Present Tense	
I am	We are
You are	They are
He/She/It is	

They <u>is</u> hungry. ✗

They <u>are</u> hungry. ✓

Past Tense	
I was	
You were	We were
He/She/It was	They were

We <u>was</u> planning a party. ✗

We <u>were</u> planning a party. ✓

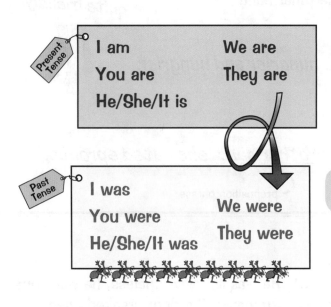

Standard and Non-Standard English

Verbs might seem pretty straightforward, but unfortunately, there are always a couple of tricksters. There are a few traps you can fall into when it comes to verbs, especially 'have', so watch out...

Don't get the two types of past tense mixed up

You usually need 'have' or 'has' with 'been' or 'done'. For more on this, see p.8.

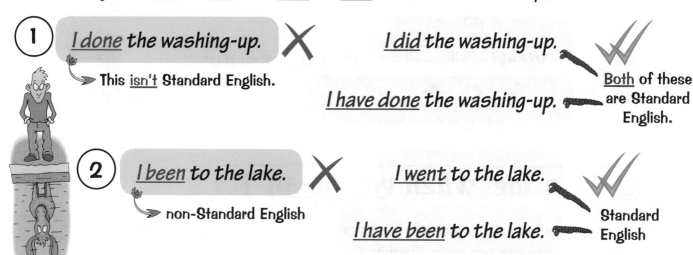

(1) **I done the washing-up.** ✗

> This isn't Standard English.

I did the washing-up. ✔✔

I have done the washing-up. ✔✔

Both of these are Standard English.

(2) **I been to the lake.** ✗

> non-Standard English

I went to the lake. ✔✔

I have been to the lake. ✔

Standard English

Use 'have' not 'of'

Don't use words like 'should' or 'could' with 'of' — it's non-Standard English.

1) It's easy to write 'of' when you mean 'have'.

John could of run faster. ✗   **John could have run faster.** ✔

2) When you use these verbs, use 'have' and never use 'of'.

I should have left.

We may have come last.

Sam must have given up.

may	will
might	could
should	shall
would	must

Quick Questions...

Rewrite each sentence so it's in Standard English. Keep the sentences in the same tense.
1) I hates sprouts.
2) He do his homework.
3) They was thirsty.
4) I is late for school.
5) They been on holiday.
6) Jack might of wanted an ice lolly.

Standard and Non-Standard English

Here's a page I prepared earlier about <u>pronouns</u>. I love <u>pronouns</u>...

Make sure every <u>pronoun</u> fits the sentence

Pronouns <u>change</u> depending on whether they're the <u>subject</u> or the <u>object</u>. In active sentences, <u>subject</u> pronouns <u>do</u> the action. An <u>object</u> pronoun has the action <u>done to it</u>. See p.3.

 *We hid really well.*   *He couldn't find us.*

This pronoun is the <u>subject</u> of the sentence.

This is the <u>object</u>.

Don't use 'me' when you mean 'I'

1) 'I' and 'me' can be tricky to get right if they're used with another <u>name</u>.
2) <u>Split</u> the sentence into <u>two parts</u>, like this:

> 'I' is always the <u>subject</u>. 'Me' is always the <u>object</u>.

Sarah and me waited for the bus.

Sarah waited for the bus. ✓   *Me waited for the bus.* ✗

This is how the sentence should be written.

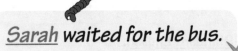 *Sarah and I waited for the bus.* ✓

Don't confuse 'them' and 'those'

'<u>Them</u>' is a <u>pronoun</u> and '<u>those</u>' <u>points something out</u>. Don't mix them up.

Them divers taste delicious.   *Those divers taste delicious.*

pronoun + noun → 'Them' <u>replaces</u> the noun, so you can't have the pronoun (them) <u>and</u> the noun (divers) in the <u>same sentence</u>.

Quick Questions...

In each of these sentences there's a mistake. Rewrite each sentence correctly.
1) I haven't met he.
2) I really want them cakes.
3) Gabriel and me went climbing.
4) He annoyed Jo and I.
5) Them books are funny.
6) Us aren't on the list.

Formal and Informal Language

Nearly there. This is the last page to learn in this section — hurrah. I've saved the best 'til last, so here's a thrilling page on formal and informal language. (It's not really thrilling — sorry.)

Formal and informal texts use different words

You can usually tell the difference between a formal text and an informal one pretty easily.

1) Formal writing uses more complicated words:

> I asked for the salad.

> I requested the salad.

'Requested' is more complicated than 'asked for'

2) Informal writing sometimes uses question tags (see p.18):

> You're coming later, aren't you?

This is a question tag.

This sentence also uses contractions — 'you're' and 'aren't' (see p.33). Formal writing doesn't use these.

Formal texts might use the subjunctive form

1) Here's another thing that's different about formal texts — when a sentence is talking about something important or urgent, it might use the subjunctive form.

INFORMAL FORM → She must make sure she buys a cat.

SUBJUNCTIVE FORM → It is essential that she buy a cat.

INFORMAL FORM → It's important that we are quiet.

SUBJUNCTIVE FORM → It is essential that we be quiet.

2) You might also see the subjunctive in sentences where the writer is talking about a situation that isn't real:

INFORMAL FORM → If I was a good waiter, I'd never drop anything.

If I were a good waiter, I would never drop anything. ← SUBJUNCTIVE FORM

Quick Questions...

Write down whether each of the sentences below is formal or informal.
1) It is vital that she learn to play chess.
2) You know my mate Barney, don't you?
3) I disagree wholeheartedly with your theory.
4) If I were allergic to eggs, I would not eat them.

Test-Style Questions

There'll be questions about <u>sentences and Standard English</u> in your <u>English SAT</u>, but it's <u>nothing</u> to worry about as long as you've done <u>lots of practice</u>. Try these <u>questions</u> to see if you're a <u>pro</u>.

Here's a Practice Question

Here's <u>how</u> to tackle a SAT-style question about <u>types of sentence</u>:

1. Tick the **two** sentences which are **statements**. ← *This tells you what you need to do.*

   Statements always end in a full stop.

   Tick two.

   I went to the shops after school. ✓

   This is a command.

   Which games do you like to play? ☐

   Listen to me! ☐ *This is a question — it ends in a question mark.*

   She is nine years old. ✓

   Here's the other statement.

   Please do not eat in here. ☐ *This ends in a full stop, but it's a command.*

Test-Style Questions

Answer these <u>SAT-style</u> questions and see how you do.

Nope, can't find them here... Answers must be on p.66.

1. Write a **question** beginning with the word given below.

   When _____

2. Look at the table below. Change the question into a **command**. Write the command in the right-hand column.

Question	Command
Can you lay the table?	

Test-Style Questions

3. Look at the table below. Put a tick in each row to show whether the words in bold make up a **phrase** or a **clause**.

Sentence	Phrase	Clause
Jesse was sitting on the step.		
I jumped **up and down all day**.		
Yesterday afternoon I played outside.		
They ate the whole pizza in an hour.		

4. Read the sentence below and circle the **conjunction**.

We waited until the clock struck twelve to have our feast.

5. Read the sentences below. Circle the correct form of the **verb** in brackets to complete each sentence.

I ___(go / goes)___ to school on the bus with my friend.

Stefan and Carlos ___(is / are)___ always fighting.

We ___(has / have)___ two rabbits and three guinea pigs.

6. Fill in the gap in the sentence below so that it uses the subjunctive form.

If she _____ faster, she would have won the race.

Sentence Punctuation

You <u>can't</u> just have a <u>load of sentences</u> without anything to <u>split them up</u> — it'd <u>sound</u> really <u>weird</u>. That's where <u>capital letters</u> and <u>full stops</u> come in <u>handy</u> — they help to <u>break up chunks of text</u>.

New sentences *start with a capital letter*

<u>Every sentence</u> has to <u>start</u> with a <u>capital letter</u>.

<u>H</u>e wanted to catch a big fish. <u>T</u>he lake was very calm.

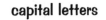 capital letters

Some words *always start with a capital letter*

Some words start with a <u>capital letter</u>, even in the <u>middle of a sentence</u>:

1) <u>Proper nouns</u> always <u>start</u> with a <u>capital letter</u>. For more on <u>proper nouns</u>, see p.1.

<u>H</u>arry and <u>Mr H</u>oward were good at finding worms.

Proper nouns are things like <u>names</u>, <u>places</u>, <u>days</u> and <u>months</u>.

<u>B</u>arcelona is in <u>S</u>pain.

Tennis club starts on the first <u>T</u>uesday in <u>M</u>arch.

2) '<u>I</u>' is <u>always</u> written with a <u>capital letter</u>, no matter where it is in a sentence.

<u>I</u> love swimming. Next year <u>I</u>'m going to Australia to go diving.

Full stops *finish sentences*

Use a <u>full stop</u> to show where a sentence <u>ends</u>. See p.18-19 for more about <u>types of sentence</u>.

I went to the park to play cricket<u>.</u> My team won by two runs<u>.</u>

 full stops

Sentence Punctuation

You can use <u>exclamation marks</u> to end a sentence too. So many decisions...

Exclamation marks <u>show</u> strong feelings

This is an <u>exclamation mark</u>: **!**

An <u>exclamation mark</u> replaces the <u>full stop</u> in sentences which show <u>strong feelings</u>.

> *Stop it<u>!</u>*

> *He was really mean<u>!</u>*

> *I couldn't believe it<u>!</u>*

> *It was fun<u>!</u>*

Some golden rules for exclamation marks

Learn these rules about <u>exclamation marks</u> and you'll be an exclamation mark <u>pro</u>.

When to use an exclamation mark:

1) For strong <u>commands</u>.
2) For someone <u>shouting</u>.
3) To show <u>surprise</u> or <u>anger</u>.

> See p.19 for more on <u>commands</u>!

When not to use an exclamation mark:

1) In <u>formal</u> writing.
2) At the <u>same time</u> as a <u>full stop</u>.

<u>Never</u> use <u>more than one</u> exclamation mark at the end of a sentence.

> *He had birds in his hair<u>!</u>* ✓

This has an <u>exclamation mark</u> because it shows <u>surprise</u>.

> *Don't eat that cake<u>!</u>* ✓

This needs an <u>exclamation mark</u> because it's a <u>command</u>.

> *He had blonde hair!* ✗

If it's <u>a statement</u>, you should use a <u>full stop</u>.

> *Don't eat that cake!!!* ✗

You only need to use <u>one</u> exclamation mark.

Sentence Punctuation

Bet you can't guess what a <u>question</u> mark is used for...

Question marks *show the end of a question*

This is a <u>question mark</u>: **?**

All <u>questions</u> need a <u>question mark</u> at the <u>end</u>:

Where shall we go<u>?</u>

Why are you hiding<u>?</u>

Most questions start with a <u>question word</u>, like '<u>where</u>' or '<u>why</u>'.
See p.18 for more on question words.

<u>Not all</u> questions start with a '<u>question word</u>' though.

Do you want some chocolate-covered caterpillars?

Watch out — some sentences just tell you <u>about a question</u>, but <u>don't</u> actually <u>ask one</u>:

Aadi asked me what I wanted for dinner.

You <u>don't</u> need a
question mark here.

An *ellipsis* **is sometimes** *useful too*

You might see '...' at the end of a sentence. This is called an '<u>ellipsis</u>' (the <u>plural</u> is 'ellips<u>es</u>').
Ellipses <u>add suspense</u> because they <u>leave the sentence unfinished</u>:

  He didn't know what to do, but then suddenly...

You can also use ellipses to show <u>interrupted speech</u>:

"Well... erm... I was just wondering..."

If only there was
more info on speech
on p.36-37...

Quick Questions...

Write out these sentences with the most suitable punctuation and capital letters.

1) on fridays i go to manchester
2) what does david like to eat
3) mrs jones asked me if i wanted a new book
4) i can't believe he just ate a slug

Apostrophes

Some people are always looking for ways to make things _easier_ for themselves. _Joining_ two words together with an _apostrophe_ is one way...

Apostrophes _join_ two words _together_

This is an _apostrophe_:  **'**

> Contractions are only for _informal writing_.

1) When you _join two words_ together, put an _apostrophe_ in to show where you've _missed out letters_. Here are some _key words_ that you _need to know_ before you get started:

CONTRACTION: the _new word_ made by _joining_ two words together.

OMISSION: when you _replace missing letters_ in a contraction with an _apostrophe_.

I am — I'm
we are — we're
do not — don't
who is — who's
does not — doesn't

I _do not_ know what _we are_ going to do.

I _don't_ know what _we're_ going to do.

Contractions use _apostrophes of omission_.

2) Some _more contractions_:

I will → I'll

I would / I had → I'd

I have → I've

let us → let's

> Contractions can also be called the '_contracted form_'.

3) Some contractions are a _bit different_:

'_I won't_' doesn't quite match the missing letters from '_I will not_'. →

I will not → I won't

cannot → can't

← 'Can't' is a _shorter_ version of just _one word_.

Think _about_ whether you need _an apostrophe_

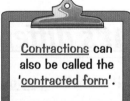

Don't use an apostrophe for talking about _more than one_ of something:

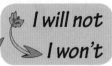 She has two pet _pig's_. ✗

 She has two pet _pigs_. ✓

Apostrophes

And here's <u>another way</u> to use <u>apostrophes</u>. Lucky you...

Apostrophes show something belongs

To show <u>possession</u>, you add an <u>apostrophe</u> and an '<u>s</u>' to the <u>owner</u> or the <u>owner's name</u>.

These apostrophes are called <u>apostrophes of possession</u>.

Eva'<u>s</u> rabbit loves carrots.

the boy'<u>s</u> computer

The computer that belongs to the boy.

The screen that belongs to the computer.

the computer'<u>s</u> screen

Even if the word <u>ends in</u> '<u>s</u>', you do the <u>same</u>:

The cactus'<u>s</u> flowers are pink.

Marcus'<u>s</u> curry was too spicy for him.

It's different for groups of people or things

If something <u>belongs</u> to a <u>group of people or things</u>, follow these rules:

(1) If the plural word <u>ends</u> in an '<u>s</u>', <u>just</u> add an <u>apostrophe</u>.

The apostrophe <u>after</u> the '<u>s</u>' shows that there's <u>more than one neighbour</u>.

Did you see the neighbours' new car?

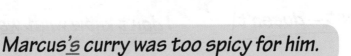

The babies' outfits always matched.

(2) If the plural word <u>doesn't end</u> in an '<u>s</u>', add an <u>apostrophe</u> and an '<u>s</u>'.

The children'<u>s</u> new hula hoops are great.

Words like '<u>men</u>' and '<u>women</u>' are the same — just add an <u>apostrophe</u> and an '<u>s</u>'.

Apostrophes

'It's' and 'its' confuse people all the time. Learn this page and make sure you're not one of those poor confused souls.

'It's' means 'it is' or 'it has'

'It's' is a contraction of 'it is' or 'it has'.

> It is very cold outside.   It's very cold outside.

> It has been a fun day.   It's been a fun day.

'Its' means 'belonging to it'

'Its' is used in the same way as 'his' or 'her'. It shows possession.

> Have you seen its feet?   is just like saying...   Have you seen her feet?

You don't need an apostrophe here.

So 'her' in this sentence can be replaced with 'its'.

'Its' doesn't always replace 'his' or 'her' though:

> Paris is famous for its museums.   This means 'the museums of Paris'.

Check you've used 'its' or 'it's' correctly

THE GOLDEN RULE

Can you replace 'it's' with 'it is' or 'it has'?
If the answer is 'yes', leave it as 'it's'.
If your answer is 'no', change it to 'its'.

'It is' or 'it has' don't make sense in this sentence.

EXAMPLE

> The dog ate it's food. ✗

> The dog ate its food. ✓

Quick Questions...

The apostrophe is wrong in each of these phrases. Write out each phrase correctly.

1) the school and it's pupils
2) Beckys' puppy
3) Iv'e
4) theyr'e
5) the fairie's wings
6) the buss' driver
7) it's legs
8) wo'nt

Inverted Commas

You might need to write some <u>speech</u>. Unfortunately that means learning how to use <u>inverted commas</u>, but they're <u>not that tricky</u>, I promise...

Inverted commas *show someone is* speaking

These are <u>inverted commas</u>: " "

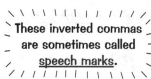
These inverted commas are sometimes called <u>speech marks</u>.

1) <u>Inverted commas</u> go around the <u>actual words</u> that <u>someone says</u>.

2) Use a <u>capital letter</u> when someone <u>starts</u> to speak.

EXAMPLE

Put a <u>capital letter</u> here.

Nick said, "Catching butterflies is sometimes tricky."

Inverted commas go at the <u>start and end</u> of speech.

Speech always *ends* with a *punctuation mark*

<u>Speech ends</u> with a <u>comma</u>, <u>full stop</u>, <u>exclamation mark</u> or <u>question mark</u>.

1) If the sentence <u>ends</u> when the speech ends, use a <u>full stop</u>:

You need a <u>comma before</u> the <u>speech starts</u>.

Josh said, "I'm really hungry."

2) If the sentence <u>carries on</u> after the speech, put a <u>comma</u> (unless it's a question or exclamation):

"We should buy some cheese," said Tom.

3) If the speech shows <u>strong feelings</u>, end it with an <u>exclamation mark</u>:

"Stop what you're doing!" shouted the police officer.

4) If the speech is a <u>question</u>, use a <u>question mark</u>:

Ravi asked, "Can we go home yet?"

Inverted Commas

Now you know how to use <u>inverted commas</u> for <u>speech</u>, it's time to learn about the <u>two different types of speech</u>. Take your time and <u>learn both</u> types — they're great fun...

Direct speech _is the exact words_ _someone says_

<u>Direct speech</u> is the stuff you just learnt about on p.36. It's when you write down the <u>exact words that someone says</u>. Have a look at this <u>example</u>:

Finn

I'm going to turn you all into soup!

These are the <u>actual words</u> that <u>Finn says</u> so you need to use <u>inverted commas</u>.

Finn shouted, "I'm going to turn you all into soup!"

Remember to put a <u>comma</u> here.

Don't forget to use the <u>correct punctuation</u> at the end of the speech.

Reported speech _is what someone has said_

<u>Reported speech</u> is writing what someone <u>has said</u> in your <u>own</u> words.

<u>Don't</u> use <u>inverted commas</u> (speech marks) for reported speech.

DIRECT SPEECH

Ed said, "I don't understand basketball."

REPORTED SPEECH

Ed said that he didn't understand basketball.

The <u>tense changes</u> for <u>reported speech</u>. 'Don't' (<u>present</u> tense) changes to 'didn't' (<u>past</u> tense) because you're <u>reporting</u> something that's <u>already been said</u>. For more on <u>verb tenses</u>, see p.7.

Quick Questions...

Write out these sentences with the correct punctuation.
1) Jay said that he didn't like apples
2) Abi said I'm bored
3) I hate you all shouted the boy
4) Where is the station asked Imogen

Commas

Commas break up a sentence — fact. They also help it <u>make more sense</u>. <u>Learn this page</u>.

Commas go between items in a list

This is a <u>comma</u>:  **,**

You use <u>commas</u> to <u>separate things</u> in a list. Get to grips with these <u>rules</u> — they're <u>pretty easy</u>.

> 1) Put a <u>comma</u> after each item in the list <u>except the last two</u>.
> 2) Put '<u>and</u>' or '<u>or</u>' between the last two items.

'<u>And</u>' <u>separates</u> the <u>last two</u> things in the list.

Pete bought a hat, boots, a scarf <u>and</u> a pair of gloves.

The commas go <u>between the items</u>, <u>not</u> each word.

Would you like to go swimming, climbing, cycling <u>or</u> sailing?

The <u>comma</u> goes <u>after</u> all these <u>except</u> the <u>last two</u>.
'<u>Or</u>' goes between the <u>last two</u> things in the list.

This rule works for <u>lists of adjectives</u> too — as long as they're about the <u>same thing</u>:

The <u>comma</u> goes <u>after</u> each adjective <u>except</u> the <u>last two</u>.

The hippo was huge, greedy, smelly <u>and</u> dangerous.

Check your commas are in the correct place

If you can <u>replace</u> all the <u>commas</u> in a list with '<u>and</u>' or '<u>or</u>', you know they're <u>correct</u>:

Pete bought a hat <u>and</u> boots <u>and</u> a scarf <u>and</u> a pair of gloves. ✓

This <u>still makes sense</u> when all the <u>commas</u> are <u>replaced</u> with '<u>and</u>', so the commas are in the <u>correct place</u>.

Commas

More ways to use commas for you — you're a lucky one today...

Commas *join* two points

You can use a comma with a conjunction to join two sentences together.

1) Take two sentences which are about the same thing:

> I like climbing.

> I'm not very good at it.

These are some conjunctions. See p.22-23 for more.

so   and   but   yet   or

2) Choose the correct linking word (conjunction):

> I like climbing.   but   I'm not very good at it.

For more on clauses, see p.20-21.

3) Whack in a comma before the linking word, and... hey presto!

> I like climbing, but I'm not very good at it.

COMPOUND SENTENCE

Commas *separate* clauses

Commas sometimes separate main clauses from subordinate clauses in a complex sentence. When the subordinate clause comes first, you use a comma to separate the clauses.

'Even though it was raining' is a subordinate clause. It doesn't make sense as a sentence on its own.

This is the main clause in the sentence. If you took away the other clause, this would still make sense.

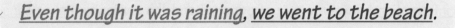

> Even though it was raining, we went to the beach.

For more on complex sentences, see p.21.

COMPLEX SENTENCE

There's a comma here to separate the two clauses.

The subordinate clause doesn't make sense on its own.

> Once I'd eaten my ice cream, I went home.

subordinate clause   comma   main clause

Commas

You'll be pleased to know that this is the <u>last page on commas</u> you need to learn. <u>Phew</u>.

Commas <u>help you add extra information</u>

1) A <u>pair</u> of commas can separate <u>extra information</u> in the middle of a sentence — they go <u>either side</u> of the extra information. Take this <u>simple sentence</u>, for example:

Susannah's crocodile is always happy.

<u>Commas</u> that help you add <u>extra information</u> work in a similar way to <u>brackets</u> and <u>dashes</u>. See p.41.

comma

Susannah's crocodile, <u>who loves flowers</u>, is always happy.

The bit <u>between the pair of commas</u> is <u>extra information</u> — it <u>doesn't make sense</u> on its own.

2) Commas are also used to join an <u>adverbial phrase</u> (see page 12) to the beginning of a sentence:

'After lunch' is an <u>adverbial phrase</u>.

<u>After lunch</u>, Susannah's crocodile is always happy.

comma

Check <u>you've used commas</u> <u>correctly</u>

There's a <u>dead easy</u> way to <u>check</u> your <u>commas</u>. Your <u>commas</u> are <u>correct</u> if you can:

1) <u>Remove</u> the <u>subordinate clause</u> and <u>comma</u> and the sentence <u>still makes sense</u>:

<u>When the park closed</u>, we were sad. ▷ *We were sad.*

The information <u>after the comma makes sense</u> on its own, so the <u>comma</u> is in the <u>right place</u>.

2) <u>Remove</u> the <u>extra information</u> between a <u>pair of commas</u> and the sentence <u>makes sense</u>:

The fish, <u>which had enormous teeth</u>, ate the worm.

The fish ate the worm.

This sentence <u>still makes sense</u> once you've <u>removed</u> the <u>extra information</u> and the <u>pair of commas</u>. That means the <u>commas</u> are in the <u>right place</u>.

Quick Questions...

<u>More</u> commas — lucky you. Write out these sentences with commas in the correct places.
1) When the bell rang I packed up my things.
2) I love cakes so I often bake cupcakes.
3) Billy my best friend is grumpy.
4) He was short rude stupid and annoying.

Brackets, Dashes and Hyphens

Brackets and dashes are a bit like pairs of commas that contain extra information.

Brackets separate extra information

These are brackets: ➡ **( )**

Brackets are also called 'parentheses'. They're always used in pairs.

Brackets go around extra information and keep it separate from the rest of the sentence.

Marco (a farmer) had lost a sheep.

You could take out the extra information in the brackets and the sentence would still make sense.

It had escaped from the field (through a gap in the fence).

This gives an explanation but doesn't affect how you read the rest of the sentence.

Dashes are similar to brackets

A pair of dashes can be used instead of brackets to add extra information:

The dogs — Tess and Bob — loved playing fetch.

This is the extra information.

A single dash can mark a pause in the middle of a sentence. It usually separates two main clauses.

Oti looked over the bridge — there was a huge drop.

dramatic pause

Use hyphens to avoid confusion

Hyphens can be used to show which word an adjective describes. They help to avoid confusion.

a long-running race

The hyphen here shows that the word 'long' describes the word 'running'. This means that the race has been running for a long time.

a long running-race

This hyphen shows that 'long' describes the words 'running-race'. This means the race is a long distance.

Quick Questions...

For each question, write out the sentence that uses brackets or dashes correctly.
1) a) (I woke up late today) after midday.   b) I woke up late today (after midday).
2) a) The pigs — Milo and Tim — like ants.   b) The pigs Milo and Tim — like ants.

Colons

Colons are really good for introducing new information — they can be tricky, but learn this page well and you'll be off to a great start.

Colons _can introduce a_ list

This is a colon:  **:**

If you're writing a list, a colon shows that the list is about to begin.

I need these ingredients for the cake:
2 eggs, 100g sugar, 100g butter,
100g flour and a big bar of chocolate.

This introduces the list of ingredients.

For more on commas, see p.38.

Only use a colon to introduce a list if it follows a main clause (see p.20-21 for more on clauses):

This is what you need to mend a puncture: a bucket
of water, scissors and a puncture repair kit.

'This is what you need to mend a puncture' is a main clause because it makes sense on its own.

If you said 'I need a bucket of water, scissors and a puncture repair kit', you wouldn't need a colon because 'I need' isn't a main clause.

Colons _can go_ before bullet points

A colon can be used to introduce a list of bullet points.
Bullet points break up information into separate points in a list.

A colon is used here to introduce the list of attractions at Spark Zoo.

You can also put commas or semi-colons at the end of each bullet point, with a full stop after the final point.

If you use a capital letter at the start of one point, then use capitals at the start of all of the points.

Come to Spark Zoo! Here are some of
our attractions:
- _A large collection of lions and tigers_
- _Rare breeds of parrot, including_
  'Sally the Singing Parrot'
- _The UK's biggest playground_

Spark Zoo

Colons

Colons are also <u>useful</u> if you want to show that you're about to <u>explain</u> something <u>in more detail</u>.

Colons introduce explanations

Colons show that you're about to <u>explain a point</u> you've <u>just made</u>:

This first bit in purple <u>tells you something</u>.

The <u>colon</u> goes <u>before the explanation</u>.

The frog was feeling very full: he'd eaten twenty-three flies.

This second bit <u>explains the first part</u> — it <u>tells you why</u> the frog was feeling very full.

Colons join together two main clauses

It can be <u>tricky</u> to know <u>when to use a colon</u>, so <u>stop and think</u> about whether your sentence actually needs one. Remember this <u>golden rule</u>:

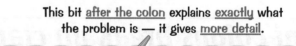

first point: more specific point

See pages 20-21 for more about <u>clauses</u>.

This is always about the <u>same thing</u> as the <u>first point</u>. It gives <u>more information</u> or an <u>explanation</u>.

This bit <u>after the colon</u> explains <u>exactly</u> what the problem is — it gives <u>more detail</u>.

Milo had a problem: he didn't know how to sit on the chair.

When they're used for <u>explanations</u>, colons normally join together <u>two main clauses</u>:

This weekend I'm going on a trip: I'm going to visit the beach.

This is the <u>main clause</u>...

...and this is another <u>main clause</u>.

Quick Questions...

Copy and complete these sentences by adding a colon in the correct place.
1) I need these things to make the salad lettuce, cucumber and tomato.
2) My neighbour has two pets her cat is called Mavis and her dog is called Otis.

Semi-Colons

Semi-colons — like half a colon. Well not really, but here's where you <u>learn</u> what they actually are. <u>Take your time</u> with semi-colons, they're <u>not the easiest punctuation mark</u> in the section.

Semi-colons break up lists

<u>Semi-colons</u> break up <u>lists</u> of <u>long phrases or clauses</u>. Unlike <u>commas</u>, you still need to put a semi-colon <u>before</u> the '<u>and</u>' or '<u>or</u>' that joins the <u>last two things</u>.

When we were in France, we played table tennis; we went to a cheese factory; I bought some posh chocolate; and my brother broke our tent.

The <u>semi-colons break up</u> the list and make it <u>easier to read</u>.

<u>Semi-colons</u> break up <u>lists</u> with <u>other punctuation marks</u> in them:

At the theme park, the girls went on a huge roller coaster; they ate ice cream at the café, which was really busy; they won a goldfish (called Jake); and they bought lots of silly, funny gifts for their friends.

Some of these clauses <u>already</u> have <u>commas</u> or <u>brackets</u> in them.

Semi-colons break up clauses in a sentence

<u>Semi-colons</u> are used to turn two <u>related main clauses</u> into <u>one sentence</u>. Both clauses must be about the <u>same</u> thing and <u>equally important</u>. They must also <u>make sense</u> on their <u>own</u>.

See pages 20-21 for more about <u>clauses</u>.

Ricky had spinach for dinner; Leo had an entire cake.

Both clauses are <u>equally important</u> and they're both about the <u>same thing</u>.

Olly was getting tired; the elephant kept struggling.

These clauses could also be written as <u>two separate sentences</u>.

Semi-Colons

They're not the easiest two punctuation marks, but try not to confuse colons and semi-colons...

Colons and semi-colons are different

Learn these rules about colons and semi-colons and you'll find them a bit easier to deal with.

COLON
1) A colon introduces a list.
2) A colon introduces an explanation or more specific information.

SEMI-COLON
1) A semi-colon is like a strong version of a comma in lists.
2) A semi-colon connects two equally important sentences.

Chris was baking a cake: a carrot cake.

This has a colon because it's giving more specific information.

These sentences are equally important but the second part doesn't explain the first part.

Chris was baking a cake; Claire was tidying up.

Punctuation can change the meaning

Look at these examples which use the same words — one has a colon and one has a semi-colon.

COLON
The mouse was playing: the cat was asleep.

The colon shows that the mouse was playing because the cat was asleep. The second part explains the first part.

SEMI-COLON
The mouse was playing; the cat was asleep.

The semi-colon shows that both parts of the sentence are related, and happening at the same time. It doesn't explain why the mouse was playing though.

Quick Questions...

Check you've got semi-colons sorted. Write these sentences with semi-colons in the right places.
1) At the park, I went down the slide I had a picnic, which was tasty and I played cricket.
2) Melissa counted the money they had raised Catherine collected the empty cake boxes.

Test-Style Questions

You'll get asked about <u>punctuation</u> in your <u>English SAT</u>, but there's no need to panic.
Try <u>these questions</u> for size and don't get in a pickle with all those <u>dots and squiggles</u>.

Here's a Practice Question

Here's <u>how</u> to tackle a SAT-style <u>punctuation question</u>.

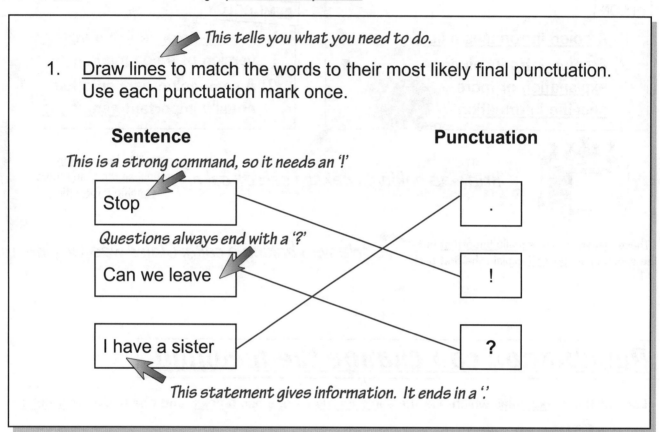

This tells you what you need to do.

1. <u>Draw lines</u> to match the words to their most likely final punctuation.
   Use each punctuation mark once.

Sentence **Punctuation**

This is a strong command, so it needs an '!'

Stop

Questions always end with a '?'

Can we leave

I have a sister

.

!

?

This statement gives information. It ends in a '.'

Test-Style Questions

The answers
are on p.67.

Have a go at these <u>SAT-style</u> questions.

1. The sentence below is missing a **comma**.
   Tick **one** box to show where the comma should go.

   Georgie shouted angrily "Get away from me!"

Test-Style Questions

2. Read the passage below. Insert **capital letters** and **full stops** so that the passage is punctuated correctly.
    One has already been done for you.

    Y
    ~~y~~esterday i was really cold mrs hatton still made
    me go outside and play tennis

3. Look at the table below. Put a tick in each row to show whether each **apostrophe** is used for **omission** or **possession**.

Sentence	Omission	Possession
The men's shoes are in the garage.		
My train's running late again.		
The teacher marked the pupils' books.		

4. Read the sentences below.
    Tick the sentence which is punctuated correctly.

    The eggs looked strange they were: square. ☐

    The eggs looked: strange they were square. ☐

    The eggs looked strange: they were square. ☐

    The eggs looked strange they: were square. ☐

5. Read the sentence below. Insert the missing **inverted commas** so that the sentence is punctuated correctly.

    After the cinema, said Hugo, shall we go for a pizza?

Plurals

A plural means more than one of something. Learn all these lovely rules about making things plural.

Add an 's' to make most things plural

With most words, just add an 's' to make them plural:

pig → pigs   banana → bananas

Some plurals are a bit different...

Here are some rules for plurals that don't follow the 'add s' rule. Watch out for exceptions...

ADD 'ES' TO WORDS ENDING IN 'CH', 'SH', 'S', 'X' AND 'Z'

If the singular word ends in a buzzing or hissing noise, you need to add 'es':

pass → passes   fox → foxes   watch → watches

FOR WORDS ENDING IN 'O', ADD 'S' OR 'ES'

Some words ending in 'o' have an 's' at the end when they're plural:

zoo → zoos   disco → discos   piano → pianos

...but some have an 'es' at the end:

hero → heroes   tomato → tomatoes

WORDS THAT END IN 'Y' SOMETIMES END IN 'IES'

Vowels are 'a', 'e', 'i', 'o' and 'u'. All the other letters are consonants.

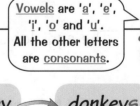

If the letter before the 'y' is a vowel, just add an 's':

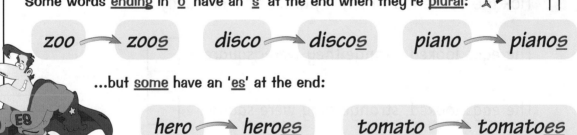

boy → boys   day → days   donkey → donkeys

But if the letter before the 'y' is a consonant, remove the 'y' and add 'ies':

berry → berries   spy → spies   puppy → puppies

Plurals

Some <u>more plurals</u> for you — I bet that'll put a <u>smile</u> on your face...

More different plural examples...

You need to <u>learn</u> these <u>irregular plurals</u>. Unfortunately the English language is full of <u>exceptions</u>.

ADD '<u>VES</u>' TO SOME WORDS <u>ENDING</u> IN '<u>F</u>' OR '<u>FE</u>'

When a word <u>ends</u> in '<u>f</u>' or '<u>fe</u>', you often need to put '<u>ves</u>' on the end:

wolf ➜ wol<u>ves</u>   wife ➜ wi<u>ves</u>   shelf ➜ shel<u>ves</u>

But <u>some</u> just need an '<u>s</u>':

che<u>fs</u>   cliff<u>s</u>   chief<u>s</u>   reef<u>s</u>   belief<u>s</u>

SOME <u>PLURAL</u> WORDS ARE <u>IRREGULAR</u>

All of these words <u>change their vowel sound</u> when they're made <u>plural</u>:

man ➜ m<u>e</u>n   woman ➜ wom<u>e</u>n   mouse ➜ m<u>i</u>ce

goose ➜ g<u>ee</u>se   foot ➜ f<u>ee</u>t   tooth ➜ t<u>ee</u>th

The <u>plural</u> of '<u>child</u>' is completely <u>irregular</u>:   child ➜ child<u>ren</u>

SOME PLURAL WORDS <u>DON'T CHANGE</u>

Some words <u>stay the same</u> in the <u>plural</u>:

sheep   deer   tuna   fish   moose

Quick Questions...

Phew, that's a lot of plurals to remember. Write each of these words as a plural.

1) pen	3) box	5) toy	7) pony	9) bat	11) way
2) calf	4) church	6) lady	8) sheep	10) loaf	12) kiss

Prefixes

Prefixes change the <u>meaning</u> of a word. <u>Magic</u>, eh? Read on and <u>learn</u> the truth behind their tricks.

Prefixes go at the beginning of a word

A <u>prefix</u> is a <u>letter</u> or <u>group</u> of letters that goes at the <u>beginning of a word</u> to form a <u>new word</u>. The word they're <u>attached</u> to is called the <u>root word</u>.

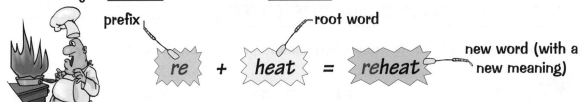

prefix — re + heat = reheat — new word (with a new meaning)

root word

Sometimes you need a <u>hyphen</u> when you add a <u>prefix</u> to a <u>root word</u> to make the <u>meaning clearer</u>:

recover — This means to get better from an illness or to get something back.

re-cover — This means to cover something again.

prefix

Prefixes can give a word an opposite meaning

<u>Prefixes</u> often make the <u>root word</u> have the <u>opposite meaning</u>. Look at these <u>examples</u>:

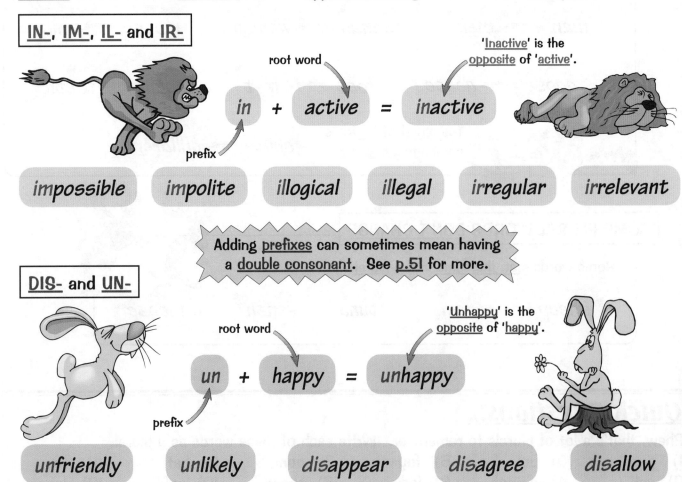

IN-, IM-, IL- and IR-

root word

'Inactive' is the <u>opposite</u> of 'active'.

in + active = inactive

prefix

impossible   impolite   illogical   illegal   irregular   irrelevant

Adding <u>prefixes</u> can sometimes mean having a <u>double consonant</u>. See <u>p.51</u> for more.

DIS- and UN-

root word

'Unhappy' is the <u>opposite</u> of 'happy'.

un + happy = unhappy

prefix

unfriendly   unlikely   disappear   disagree   disallow

Prefixes

Ahh <u>more prefixes</u> — this is the <u>last page</u> on them, I <u>promise</u>.

You need to know these common prefixes

Learn these <u>prefixes</u> and look at how they <u>change the meaning</u> of the root:

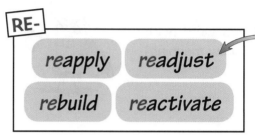

RE-

reapply readjust

rebuild reactivate

'<u>Re</u>' usually means '<u>again</u>', so '<u>readjust</u>' means '<u>adjust again</u>'.

TRANS-

transport transform

transplant transfix

'<u>Trans</u>' means '<u>across</u>', '<u>beyond</u>' or '<u>through</u>'. '<u>transport</u>' means '<u>move across a space</u>'.

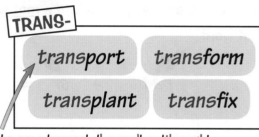

'<u>Pre</u>' means '<u>before</u>'. '<u>preheat</u>' means '<u>heat before</u>'.

PRE-

prepaid preheat

preview precaution

AUTO-

autobiography

autograph autopilot

'<u>Auto</u>' is like '<u>self</u>', e.g. an '<u>autobiography</u>' is something you write about <u>yourself</u>.

Sometimes <u>two words</u> make sense when they're <u>joined together</u>, e.g. <u>news</u>paper, <u>white</u>board, <u>farm</u>yard. These are called <u>compound words</u>.

fire**man** → '<u>Fireman</u>' is a <u>compound word</u> made from the words '<u>fire</u>' and '<u>man</u>'.

hand**writing** → If you don't know how to <u>spell</u> a <u>compound word</u>, break it up into its <u>separate</u> parts — e.g. '<u>hand</u>' and '<u>writing</u>'.

Root words don't change their spelling

I just <u>love</u> roots.

The root word <u>never changes</u> when a <u>prefix</u> is added, so <u>don't add</u> or <u>remove</u> letters. That means that sometimes you end up with a <u>double letter</u> in the word:

un + necessary → unecessary ✗

un + necessary → unnecessary ✓

ir + regular → iregular ✗

ir + regular → irregular ✓

These are <u>correct</u> because the <u>spelling</u> of the <u>root</u> word <u>hasn't changed</u>.

Quick Questions...

For each of these root words, choose the most suitable prefix.

1) (in / dis) decent 3) (il / in) literate 5) (dis / un) popular 7) (im / un) personal
2) (un / ir) resistible 4) (dis / im) patient 6) (un / dis) afraid 8) (il / in) capable

Suffixes

Suffixes change the <u>meaning</u> of a word. <u>Learn</u> this page and find out <u>how</u>...

Suffixes <u>go at the end</u> of a word

A <u>suffix</u> is a <u>letter</u> or a <u>group</u> of letters that goes at the <u>end of a word</u>.
Like prefixes, they always attach to a <u>root word</u>.

root word   suffix   new word (with a
                                        new meaning)

paint + *er* = *painter*

Suffixes <u>form</u> nouns — <u>ment, ness, er, ity</u>

A <u>suffix</u> can turn a <u>verb</u> or an <u>adjective</u> into a <u>noun</u>. '-<u>ment</u>', '-<u>ness</u>', '-<u>er</u>' and '-<u>ity</u>' all form <u>nouns</u>
(for more on nouns, see p.1-2). <u>Watch out</u> for <u>spelling changes</u> when a <u>suffix</u> is added to a word.

happy + *ness* = *happiness* ← If the root word ends in a <u>consonant</u> and
                                          a '<u>y</u>', you normally <u>change</u> the '<u>y</u>' to '<u>i</u>'.

root word   suffix   new word (<u>noun</u>)
(<u>adjective</u>)

care + *er* = *carer*

root word (<u>verb</u>)   When the root word ends in '<u>e</u>'
                              and the <u>first letter</u> of the <u>suffix</u>
                              is a <u>vowel</u>, you lose the '<u>e</u>'.

active + *ity* = *activity*

Suffixes <u>form</u> adjectives — <u>less, ful, able, ible</u>

These <u>suffixes</u> turn <u>verbs</u> and <u>nouns</u> into <u>adjectives</u>:

-LESS + -FUL

fear + *less* = *fearless*   *hope* + *ful* = *hopeful*

root word (<u>verb</u>)   suffix   new word (<u>adjective</u>)

-ABLE + -IBLE

rely + *able* = *reliable*   *reverse* + *ible* = *reversible*

Remember that '<u>y</u>' changes to '<u>i</u>' if there's a <u>consonant</u>   You <u>lose</u> the last '<u>e</u>' from '<u>reverse</u>'
before it, and the <u>suffix</u> begins with a <u>vowel</u>.   because the suffix <u>begins</u> with a <u>vowel</u>.

Suffixes

If you <u>loved</u> the <u>last page</u>, you'll <u>like</u> this page too. If you hate <u>suffixes</u>... <u>tough luck</u>, I'm afraid.

Suffixes form adverbs and verbs

Whack '<u>ly</u>' on the <u>end</u> of an <u>adjective</u> to turn it into an <u>adverb</u>. Watch out for <u>spelling changes</u>:

$$\boxed{quick} + \boxed{ly} = \boxed{quickly} \qquad \boxed{happy} + \boxed{ly} = \boxed{happily}$$

Remember that the '<u>y</u>' <u>changes</u> to '<u>i</u>'.

You can add <u>suffixes</u> to <u>nouns or adjectives</u> to form <u>verbs</u>. Have a look at these <u>examples</u>:

$$\boxed{critic} + \boxed{ise} = \boxed{criticise} \qquad \boxed{simple} + \boxed{ify} = \boxed{simplify}$$

noun   suffix   verb   adjective   suffix   verb

You need to <u>drop</u> the '<u>e</u>' here.

'ed' and 'ing' change the tense of a verb

For more on <u>verbs</u>, see p.6-9.

-ED

Use '<u>ed</u>' to put a <u>verb</u> in the <u>past tense</u>:

$$\boxed{want} + \boxed{ed} = \boxed{wanted}$$

present tense   suffix   past tense

too many 'e's

If the <u>present tense verb</u> already ends in an '<u>e</u>', <u>drop</u> one of the '<u>e</u>'s:

$$\boxed{bake} + \boxed{ed} = \boxed{baked} \checkmark \quad \boxed{bakeed} \times$$

Remember, you <u>can't</u> use '<u>ed</u>' with <u>all</u> verbs — many verbs in the <u>past tense</u> are <u>irregular</u>.

-ING

Add '<u>ing</u>' to a verb to make an <u>-ing verb</u>:

$$\boxed{want} + \boxed{ing} = \boxed{wanting}$$

present tense   suffix   -ing verb

If the <u>present tense verb</u> already ends in an '<u>e</u>', <u>lose</u> the '<u>e</u>':

$$\boxed{bake} + \boxed{ing} = \boxed{baking} \checkmark \quad \boxed{bakeing} \times$$

double consonant

Sometimes if a word <u>ends in a consonant</u>, you have to <u>double the consonant</u>:

$$\boxed{run} + \boxed{ing} = \boxed{running}$$

Quick Questions...

Turn each root word into a new word by adding the appropriate suffix. The first one's been done.

1) play (adjective) playful
2) power (adjective)
3) make (-ing verb)
4) sad (noun)
5) agree (noun)
6) bold (adverb)
7) sit (-ing verb)
8) beauty (adjective)

Homophones

Homophones can be a bit <u>confusing</u>, but learn these <u>off by heart</u>, and you'll be just <u>fine</u>...

<u>Homophones</u> **are** <u>words that</u> **sound the same**

A <u>homophone</u> is a word that <u>sounds the same</u> as <u>another word</u>, but has a <u>different meaning</u>.

They're/their/there

Make sure you <u>don't confuse</u> '<u>they're</u>', '<u>their</u>' and '<u>there</u>'. They mean three very <u>different</u> things.

1) '<u>They're</u>' is short for '<u>they are</u>'.
2) '<u>Their</u>' means it <u>belongs to them</u>.
3) '<u>There</u>' is for <u>places</u>.

<u>They're</u> really big.

<u>Their</u> tents are red.

It's over <u>there</u>.

To/too/two

<u>Mixing up</u> these three is an <u>easy mistake</u> to make. <u>Learn</u> these <u>rules</u>:

Rosie wants <u>to</u> fly.

I'm going <u>to</u> France.

They went <u>too</u>.

He eats <u>too</u> much.

He saw <u>two</u> cats.

1) '<u>To</u>' can mean '<u>towards</u>' or it can be <u>part of a verb</u>.
2) '<u>Too</u>' is like saying '<u>as well</u>' or '<u>too much</u>'.
3) '<u>Two</u>' is for the <u>number</u> — <u>2</u>.

Where/were/wear

These <u>three little troublemakers</u> aren't quite so <u>troublesome</u> when you <u>learn the rules</u> for them:

1) '<u>Where</u>' is for <u>places</u> and <u>positions</u>.
2) '<u>Were</u>' is the <u>past</u> tense of '<u>are</u>'.
3) '<u>Wear</u>' is for <u>clothes</u> and <u>jewellery</u>.

<u>Where</u> is my brother's cat?

You <u>were</u> really moody.

I <u>wear</u> a necklace and boots.

Homophones

You're in for a <u>treat</u> today — <u>another</u> page of <u>homophones</u>. <u>Hurrah</u>.

Don't write 'of' instead of 'off'

'<u>Of</u>' and '<u>off</u>' are two <u>completely different</u> words:

1) '<u>Of</u>' is a <u>preposition</u>.
2) '<u>Off</u>' is like saying '<u>away from</u>' or '<u>not on</u>'.

The bag was full <u>of</u> rubbish.

He took the bag <u>off</u> the table.

This is like saying 'he took the bag <u>away from</u> the table'.

'Passed' and 'past' mean different things

Make sure you know <u>when to use</u> '<u>passed</u>' and '<u>past</u>':

1) '<u>Passed</u>' is an action word. It's the past tense of the verb 'to pass'.
2) '<u>Past</u>' isn't an action word. It's a preposition.

I <u>passed</u> the ball.

Go <u>past</u> the park.

'Affect' is the action, 'effect' is the result

It's so easy to get '<u>affect</u>' and '<u>effect</u>' <u>mixed up</u>. Remember these <u>tips</u> and you'll <u>get 'em right</u>.

Remember:
<u>A</u>ffect =
<u>A</u>ction

AFFECT is the **ACTION** which <u>influences</u> something.

EFFECT is the **RESULT** of an action.

The mouldy cheese will <u>affect</u> my dreams.

The mouldy cheese is <u>doing an action</u>.

This talks about <u>the result</u> of eating the mouldy cheese.

The mouldy cheese had a horrible <u>effect</u>.

Quick Questions...

Write these sentences with the correct homophone.

1) Get the dog (of/off) the sofa.
2) He (past/passed) the restaurant.
3) The apple is over (there/their).
4) What (affect/effect) did it have?

Silent and Unstressed Letters

Silent letters are horrible <u>tricksters</u> — don't let them catch you out. You <u>don't</u> say these letters <u>out loud</u> when you say a <u>word</u>, but you must <u>remember</u> them when you <u>write</u> them down.

Silent 'g' and 'k' are followed by 'n'

'<u>G</u>' and '<u>k</u>' are usually silent when they are followed by '<u>n</u>'.

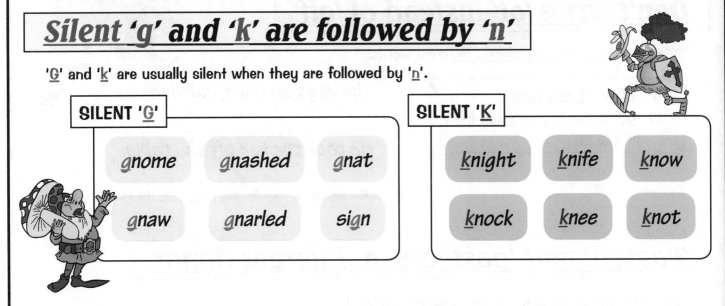

SILENT '<u>G</u>'

<u>g</u>nome	<u>g</u>nashed	<u>g</u>nat
<u>g</u>naw	<u>g</u>narled	si<u>g</u>n

SILENT '<u>K</u>'

<u>k</u>night	<u>k</u>nife	<u>k</u>now
<u>k</u>nock	<u>k</u>nee	<u>k</u>not

Letters 'l', 'h', 'w' and 'b' can be <u>silent</u> too

There's no easy <u>rule</u> for these silent letters. You just have to <u>learn</u> them I'm afraid.

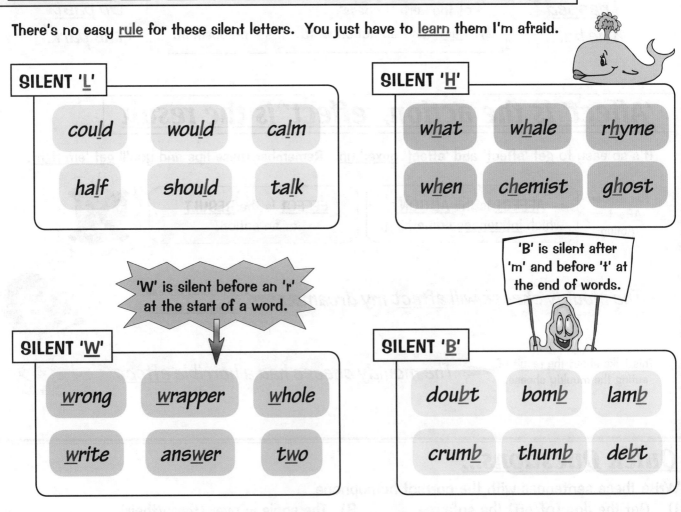

SILENT '<u>L</u>'

cou<u>l</u>d	wou<u>l</u>d	ca<u>l</u>m
ha<u>l</u>f	shou<u>l</u>d	ta<u>l</u>k

SILENT '<u>H</u>'

w<u>h</u>at	w<u>h</u>ale	r<u>h</u>yme
w<u>h</u>en	c<u>h</u>emist	g<u>h</u>ost

> 'W' is silent before an 'r' at the start of a word.

SILENT '<u>W</u>'

<u>w</u>rong	<u>w</u>rapper	<u>w</u>hole
<u>w</u>rite	ans<u>w</u>er	t<u>w</u>o

> 'B' is silent after 'm' and before 't' at the end of words.

SILENT '<u>B</u>'

dou<u>b</u>t	bom<u>b</u>	lam<u>b</u>
crum<u>b</u>	thum<u>b</u>	de<u>b</u>t

Silent and Unstressed Letters

Underlined letters aren't always silent, but they are tricky to hear when they're spoken out loud. That's why they can cause mistakes, and that's why you need to learn these spellings.

Unstressed vowels are hard to hear

Sometimes, vowels in a word sound like a different vowel.
Other times, they sound like they're not there at all.

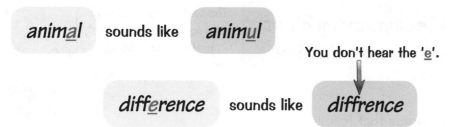

animal   sounds like   animul

You don't hear the 'e'.

difference   sounds like   diffrence

Learn these spellings with unstressed vowels

Don't let unstressed vowels stress you out — learn these commonly misspelt words.

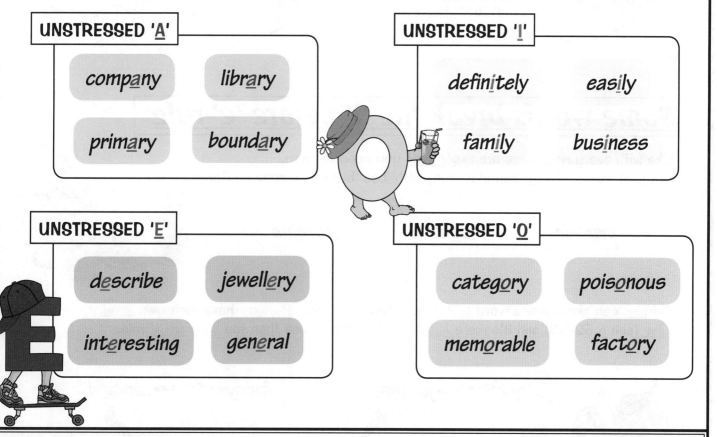

UNSTRESSED 'A'

company   library

primary   boundary

UNSTRESSED 'I'

definitely   easily

family   business

UNSTRESSED 'E'

describe   jewellery

interesting   general

UNSTRESSED 'O'

category   poisonous

memorable   factory

Quick Questions...

Write out the sentences below, filling in each gap with a silent letter or unstressed vowel.

1) The soup comp__ny is a fam__ly bus__ness.
2) I cou__d see a g__ost and a __night.
3) Ta__k to me w__en you're ca__mer.
4) Dara got t__o ans__ers __rong.

Confusing Words

'E' and 'i' often appear <u>together</u> in words, so it can be <u>difficult</u> to know which way round they're supposed to go. Learn this page and <u>master</u> the '<u>ie</u>' conundrum.

Learn the 'i' before 'e' rule

Use this <u>rule</u> to decide whether '<u>i</u>' comes <u>before</u> '<u>e</u>' or <u>after</u> it.

'i' before 'e' except after 'c' but only when it rhymes with 'bee'.

The whole word doesn't need to rhyme with 'bee', just the 'ie' sound.

Here are some <u>examples</u> of words that <u>follow the rule</u>:

bel<u>ie</u>ve   <u>Rhymes</u> with 'bee' so 'i' <u>before</u> 'e'.

rec<u>ei</u>ve   <u>Rhymes</u> with 'bee' but follows '<u>c</u>' so 'i' <u>after</u> 'e'.

n<u>ei</u>ghbour   <u>Doesn't rhyme</u> with 'bee' so 'i' <u>after</u> 'e'.

sc<u>ie</u>nce   <u>Doesn't rhyme</u> with 'bee' but follows '<u>c</u>' so 'i' <u>before</u> 'e'.

Some words break the 'i' before 'e' rule

Like with every rule, there are <u>exceptions</u> you need to learn.
In <u>these</u> words, the '<u>ie</u>' sound <u>rhymes</u> with 'bee' but the '<u>i</u>' comes after '<u>e</u>'.

prot<u>ei</u>n   **s<u>ei</u>ze**   **caff<u>ei</u>ne**

<u>Suffixes</u> can also make a word <u>break</u> the 'i before e' rule. <u>Suffixes</u> have their own <u>spelling rules</u> (see p.52-53) and it's more <u>important</u> to follow those than the '<u>i before e</u>' rule.

juicy ⟶ **jui<u>ci</u>est**   **fancy** ⟶ **fan<u>ci</u>ed**

The 'ie' comes after '<u>c</u>' because the suffix is '<u>est</u>'.

It's the same here — the suffix is '<u>ed</u>'.

Word Families

Some words belong to <u>word families</u> — groups of words that <u>look similar</u> and have <u>similar meanings</u>.

Similar words make word families

Words that are from the same <u>word family</u> look like each other — you can usually <u>spot</u> bits of each word that are the <u>same</u>. The part of the word they have in common is called a <u>root</u>.

<u>sun</u>shine   <u>sun</u>ny   <u>sun</u>screen ← These all have '<u>sun</u>' as their root.

It might be a bit <u>less obvious</u> sometimes...

 un<u>clear</u>   <u>clar</u>ify ← These words are still from the <u>same family</u> — the root is just <u>spelt differently</u>.

Word families have similar meanings

Words that are from the same <u>word family</u> will always be <u>about the same topic</u> or thing:

a<u>round</u>   sur<u>round</u>   <u>round</u>about ← These words are all to do with going <u>around</u> or <u>outside</u> of something.

<u>gra</u>cious   <u>gra</u>teful   <u>gra</u>titude ← These words are all to do with saying <u>thank you</u>.

If you <u>can't tell</u> what the <u>root</u> means straight away, you can work it out from the <u>meaning of the words</u>:

bio<u>graph</u>y   auto<u>graph</u>   para<u>graph</u> ← These words are all about things that are <u>written down</u>, so you can guess that's what the <u>root</u> means.

Quick Questions...

Write down the root for each of these word families, and say what you think it means.
1) aerial, aeroplane.
2) duplicate, duet.
3) passport, passenger.
4) ballroom, ballerina.
5) solar, parasol
6) annual, anniversary

Synonyms and Antonyms

'Synonym' might look like a scary word, but it's okay really. Learn this page and see for yourself.

Synonyms mean the same thing

You need to be able to spot synonyms and come up with your own ones too.
But don't stress — with a bit of practice, you'll be a synonym superstar in no time.

A synonym is a word that means the same or a very similar thing to another word.

SYNONYMS FOR 'SCARY'

Even the cat thought the witch was scary.

These three words (synonyms) could replace the word 'scary' and the sentence would mean the same:

terrifying   petrifying   frightening

Check your synonym fits the context

Make sure that the synonym you choose makes sense in your sentence.
Look at these examples where the word 'sad' is used in different sentences.

 Bashira was really sad. upset or distressed

Here you need a word that can describe a person.

 *The film was really sad.* tragic or upsetting

You need words to describe a film here.
You couldn't use a word like 'upset'.
The sentence wouldn't make sense.

The film was really upset.

Synonyms and Antonyms

There may well be questions on antonyms in the test. Don't worry though, they're dead easy. (Here's a clue — 'easy' is an antonym of 'difficult').

Antonyms are opposites

'Antonym' is a fancy word for 'opposite'.

Sometimes you can add a prefix to make a word an antonym. See p.50.

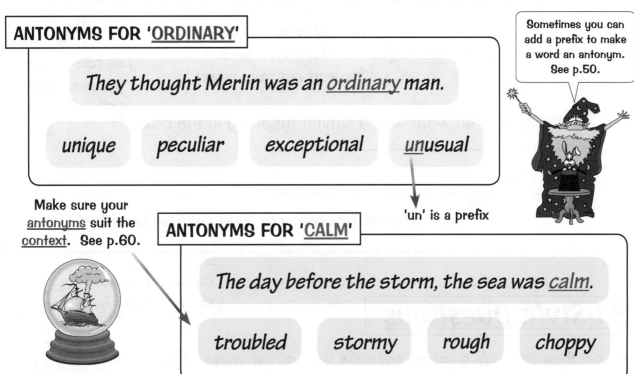

ANTONYMS FOR 'ORDINARY'

They thought Merlin was an ordinary man.

unique   peculiar   exceptional   unusual

'un' is a prefix

Make sure your antonyms suit the context. See p.60.

ANTONYMS FOR 'CALM'

The day before the storm, the sea was calm.

troubled   stormy   rough   choppy

Suffixes can make antonyms

You can also add the suffixes 'ful' and 'less' to the end of a root word to make two antonyms.

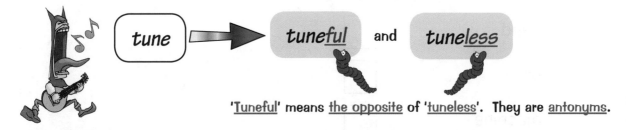

tune → tuneful and tuneless

'Tuneful' means the opposite of 'tuneless'. They are antonyms.

Quick Questions...

Find a synonym and an antonym for each underlined word in the sentences below.
1) My cousin is really rude.
2) We had to walk quickly.
3) The mansion was big.
4) He spoke very quietly.
5) His dog is ugly.
6) My party will be great.

Test-Style Questions

Those examiners do like to ask about spellings and word meanings. Luckily, all the information you need is here in Section Four. Learn all the handy tips and tricks and give these questions a whirl.

Here's a Practice Question

Here's how to tackle a SAT-style question.

1. You want to replace the word '**small**' in the sentence below.

    You need to replace this word.

    The ant was <u>small</u>. ⬅ *Read the whole sentence to work out the context.*

    This tells you what you need to do.

    Write another word with a similar meaning in the box.

tiny

    'Tiny' has a similar meaning to 'small' and fits the context.

Got to get to those answers on p.67...

Test-Style Questions

Check out these SAT-style questions and make sure you can answer them.

1. What does the root **man** mean in the word family below?

    manual   manicure   manufacture

    Tick **one** box.

    hand   ☐

    boy   ☐

    machine ☐

    main   ☐

Test-Style Questions

2.   Read the sentence below.
     Tick the word that is closest in meaning to the word '**leapt**'.

     The puppy <u>leapt</u> over the wall.

                              Tick **one** box.

     played   ☐

     jumped   ☐

     growled   ☐

     hid   ☐

3.   Put a prefix at the start of each word below to make it mean
     the **opposite**.

     _____ polite

     _____ happy

     _____ honest

4.   Read the words below.
     Tick the ending that would make the word '**care**' an **adjective**.

                              Tick **one** box.

     car**er**   ☐

     car**ed**   ☐

     care**s**   ☐

     care**ful**   ☐

Glossary

Adjective		A word that describes a noun, e.g. <u>big</u> house, <u>cold</u> morning.
Adverb		A word that describes a verb, e.g. run <u>quickly</u>, dance <u>happily</u>.
Antonym		A word that means the <u>opposite</u> to another word, e.g. <u>big</u> and <u>small</u>.
Apostrophe	'	Used to show <u>missing letters</u> (omission) and <u>belonging</u> (possession).
Article		The words <u>the</u>, <u>a</u> or <u>an</u> which go before a noun. A type of <u>determiner</u>.
Brackets	( )	Used to separate <u>extra information</u> in a sentence.
Capital letter	A	Used for <u>proper nouns</u> and for <u>starting sentences</u>.
Clause		A bit of a sentence that contains <u>a verb</u> and someone <u>doing the action</u>.
Colon	:	Used to introduce some <u>lists</u> and joins <u>sentences</u>.
Comma	,	Separates items in a <u>list</u>, separates <u>extra information</u> and <u>joins clauses</u>.
Conjunction		A word or words used to <u>link</u> two <u>clauses</u> or <u>sentences</u>, e.g. <u>and</u>, <u>however</u>.
Contraction		The <u>new word</u> made by <u>joining</u> two words together with an <u>apostrophe</u>.
Dash	—	Used to separate <u>extra information</u> in a sentence.
Determiner		A word that goes before a <u>noun</u> to tell you whether it is <u>general</u> or <u>specific</u>.
Direct speech		The <u>actual</u> words that are <u>said</u> by someone.
Exclamation mark	!	Used to show strong <u>feelings</u> and for some <u>commands</u>.
Full stop	.	Used to show where a sentence <u>ends</u>.

Glossary

Homophone Words that <u>sound the same</u> but have a <u>different meaning</u>, e.g. <u>too</u> and <u>two</u>.

Hyphen `-` Used to show which word an <u>adjective describes</u> to <u>avoid confusion</u>.

Inverted commas `" "` Used to show <u>direct speech</u>.

Main clause An <u>important</u> bit of a sentence that would <u>make sense</u> on its own, e.g. <u>I went out</u> even though it was raining. 'I went out' is the <u>main clause</u>.

Noun A word that <u>names</u> something, e.g. <u>Paul</u>, <u>scissors</u>, <u>herd</u>, <u>happiness</u>.

Phrase A <u>small part</u> of a sentence, usually <u>without a verb</u>.

Plural <u>More than one</u> of something, e.g. lots of <u>biscuits</u>, two <u>mice</u>, all his <u>teeth</u>.

Prefix <u>Letters</u> that can be put <u>in front</u> of a word to change its meaning, e.g. <u>un</u>lock.

Preposition A word that tells you <u>how</u> things are <u>related</u>, e.g. <u>in</u>, <u>above</u>, <u>before</u>.

Pronoun A word that can be used <u>instead of a noun</u>, e.g. <u>I</u>, <u>you</u>, <u>he</u>, <u>it</u>.

Question mark `?` Used at the end of <u>questions</u>.

Reported speech What someone has said, but <u>not</u> in their <u>own words</u>.

Semi-colon `;` Used to separate <u>lists</u> of longer things and <u>joins</u> sentences.

Subordinate clause A <u>less important</u> bit of a sentence which <u>doesn't make sense</u> on its own, e.g. <u>While I was out</u>, he slept. 'While I was out' is the <u>subordinate clause</u>.

Suffix Letters that can be put <u>after</u> a word to change its meaning, e.g. play<u>ful</u>.

Synonym A word with <u>the same</u> or a <u>similar meaning</u> to another word, e.g. <u>small</u> and <u>tiny</u>.

Verb A <u>doing</u> or <u>being</u> word, e.g. I <u>run</u>, he <u>went</u>, you <u>are</u>.

Answers

Section One — Grammar

Page 2

1) Kai — proper
   Brighton Pier — proper
   flock — collective
   seagulls — common
   doughnuts — common

2) superstar — common
   inspiration — abstract
   plane — common
   Barbados — proper

Page 4

1) "Dad," <u>I</u> said, "the slippers are <u>yours</u>."

2) Ganika said <u>she</u> would be late for school.

3) <u>We</u> took the parcel and hid <u>it</u> under the bed.

4) Hal has sweets <u>that</u> <u>he</u> won't share.

Page 5

1) You should have circled 'some'.

2) You should have circled 'an'.

3) You should have circled 'the' and 'my'.

4) You should have circled 'the' and 'fourteen'.

Page 7

1) The dog **eats / ate** my homework.

2) They **want / wanted** ice cream for pudding.

3) You **are** doing the washing up tonight.

4) I often **think** before I **speak**.

Page 9

1) active
2) passive
3) passive
4) passive

Page 11

1) cold, hot
2) <u>funniest</u>
3) stinky, <u>stinkiest</u>
4) unusual, green, orange

Page 13

1) The friendly aliens visit Earth <u>frequently</u>.

2) The fireworks exploded <u>extremely brightly</u>.

3) The giraffe was snoring <u>incredibly loudly</u>.

4) She worked <u>hard</u> to finish the hard sums.

Page 15

Answers will vary. For example:

1) I carry my books **in** my school bag.

2) Matt eats breakfast **before** he gets dressed.

3) I have not seen him **since** last week.

4) The car drove **under** the bridge.

Pages 16-17

1) You should have circled 'the', 'a' and 'two'.

2) You should have circled 'we'.

3) shoes — A
   oldest — C
   fit — B
   comfortably — D

4) speak — **spoke**
   tell — **told**
   is — **was**

5) Answers will vary. For example:
   The ballerina danced **gracefully** across the stage and the audience clapped **enthusiastically**.

Section Two — Sentence Grammar

Page 19

1) exclamation
2) question
3) command
4) statement
5) command
6) exclamation
7) question
8) statement

Page 21

1) main clause
2) subordinate clause
3) subordinate clause
4) main clause

Page 23

You should have underlined:

1) yet
2) because
3) Nevertheless

4) Suddenly

Page 25

1) I **hate** sprouts.
2) He **does** his homework.
3) They **were** thirsty.
4) I **am** late for school.
5) They **have been** on holiday.
6) Jack might **have** wanted an ice lolly.

Page 26

1) I haven't met **him**.
2) I really want **those / these** cakes.
3) Gabriel and **I** went climbing.
4) He annoyed **Jo and me**.
5) **Those / These** books are funny.
6) **We** aren't on the list.

Page 27

1) Formal
2) Informal
3) Formal
4) Formal

Pages 28-29

1) Answers will vary. For example:
   When are you leaving?

2) Lay the table.

3) **Jesse was sitting** on the step.
   — clause
   I jumped **up and down all day**.
   — phrase
   Yesterday afternoon I played outside. — phrase
   They ate the whole pizza in an hour.
   — clause

4) You should have circled 'until'.

5) You should have circled:
   I **go** to school on the bus with my friend.
   Stefan and Carlos **are** always fighting.
   We **have** two rabbits and three guinea pigs.

6) If she <u>were</u> faster, she would have won the race.

Section Three — Punctuation

Page 32

1) **On** Fridays **I** go to **M**anchester**.**
2) **W**hat does **D**avid like to eat**?**
3) **M**rs **J**ones asked me if **I** wanted a new book**.**

Answers

4) **I** can't believe he just ate a slug**!**

Page 35

1) the school and its pupils
2) Becky's puppy
3) I've
4) they're
5) the fairies' wings
6) the bus's driver
7) its legs
8) won't

Page 37

1) Jay said that he didn't like apples.
2) Abi said, "I'm bored."
3) "I hate you all!" shouted the boy.
4) "Where is the station?" asked Imogen.

Page 40

1) When the bell rang, I packed up my things.
2) I love cakes, so I often bake cupcakes.
3) Billy, my best friend, is grumpy.
4) He was short, rude, stupid and annoying.

Page 41

1) b) I woke up late today (after midday).
2) a) The pigs — Milo and Tim — like ants.

Page 43

1) I need these things to make the salad**:** lettuce, cucumber and tomato.
2) My neighbour has two pets**:** her cat is called Mavis and her dog is called Otis.

Page 45

1) At the park, I went down the slide**;** I had a picnic, which was tasty**;** and I played cricket.
2) Melissa counted the money they had raised**;** Catherine collected the empty cake boxes.

Pages 46-47

1) Georgie shouted angrily, "Get away from me!"

2) **Y**esterday **I** was really cold**.** **M**rs **H**atton still made me go outside and play tennis**.**
3) The men's shoes are in the garage. — possession
My train's running late again. — omission
The teacher marked the pupils' books. — possession
4) You should have ticked this sentence:
The eggs looked strange: they were square.
5) "After the cinema," said Hugo, "shall we go for a pizza?"

Section Four — Spelling

Page 49

1) pens
2) calves
3) boxes
4) churches
5) toys
6) ladies
7) ponies
8) sheep
9) bats
10) loaves
11) ways
12) kisses

Page 51

1) **in**decent
2) **ir**resistible
3) **il**literate
4) **im**patient
5) **un**popular
6) **un**afraid
7) **im**personal
8) **in**capable

Page 53

1) play**ful**
2) power**ful** / power**less**
3) mak**ing**
4) sad**ness**
5) agree**ment**
6) bold**ly**
7) sitt**ing**
8) beauti**ful**

Page 55

1) Get the dog **off** the sofa.
2) He **passed** the restaurant.
3) The apple is over **there**.
4) What **effect** did it have?

Page 57

1) The soup comp**a**ny is a fam**i**ly business.
2) I could see a g**h**ost and a **k**night.
3) Talk to me w**h**en you're calmer.
4) Dara got t**w**o answers **w**rong.

Page 58

1) The chi**e**f bel**ie**ved he would win.
2) My dad ordered the spic**ie**st curry.
3) The sci**e**ntist made a tough decision.
4) **Ei**ght pr**ie**sts went ice skating.

Page 59

1) 'aer' — to do with the air / the sky.
2) 'du' — to do with the number two.
3) 'pass' — to do with going somewhere.
4) 'ball' — to do with dancing.
5) 'sol' — to do with the sun.
6) 'ann' — to do with one year.

Page 61

Answers will vary. For example:

1) synonym: impolite
   antonym: polite
2) synonym: fast
   antonym: slowly
3) synonym: huge
   antonym: tiny
4) synonym: softly
   antonym: loudly
5) synonym: unattractive
   antonym: beautiful
6) synonym: fantastic
   antonym: terrible

Pages 62-63

1) hand
2) You should have ticked 'jumped'.
3) **im**polite
   unhappy
   dishonest
4) You should have ticked 'careful'.

Index